COLLEGE LEVEL EXAMINATION
PROGRAM SERIES

THIS IS YOUR **PASSBOOK®** FOR ...

INFORMATION SYSTEMS

NATIONAL LEARNING CORPORATION®
passbooks.com

PASSBOOK® SERIES

THE *PASSBOOK® SERIES* has been created to prepare applicants and candidates for the ultimate academic battlefield – the examination room.

At some time in our lives, each and every one of us may be required to take an examination – for validation, matriculation, admission, qualification, registration, certification, or licensure.

Based on the assumption that every applicant or candidate has met the basic formal educational standards, has taken the required number of courses, and read the necessary texts, the *PASSBOOK® SERIES* furnishes the one special preparation which may assure passing with confidence, instead of failing with insecurity. Examination questions – together with answers – are furnished as the basic vehicle for study so that the mysteries of the examination and its compounding difficulties may be eliminated or diminished by a sure method.

This book is meant to help you pass your examination provided that you qualify and are serious in your objective.

The entire field is reviewed through the huge store of content information which is succinctly presented through a provocative and challenging approach – the question-and-answer method.

A climate of success is established by furnishing the correct answers at the end of each test.

You soon learn to recognize types of questions, forms of questions, and patterns of questioning. You may even begin to anticipate expected outcomes.

You perceive that many questions are repeated or adapted so that you can gain acute insights, which may enable you to score many sure points.

You learn how to confront new questions, or types of questions, and to attack them confidently and work out the correct answers.

You note objectives and emphases, and recognize pitfalls and dangers, so that you may make positive educational adjustments.

Moreover, you are kept fully informed in relation to new concepts, methods, practices, and directions in the field.

You discover that you arre actually taking the examination all the time: you are preparing for the examination by "taking" an examination, not by reading extraneous and/or supererogatory textbooks.

In short, this PASSBOOK®, used directedly, should be an important factor in helping you to pass your test.

College-Level Examination Program (CLEP)

1. WHAT IS CLEP?

CLEP stands for the College-Level Examination Program, sponsored by the College Board. It is a national program of credit-by-examination that offers you the opportunity to obtain recognition for college-level achievement. No matter when, where, or how you have learned – by means of formal or informal study – you can take CLEP tests. If the results are acceptable to your college, you can receive credit.

You may not realize it, but you probably know more than your academic record reveals. Each day you, like most people, have an opportunity to learn. In private industry and business, as well as at all levels of government, learning opportunities continually occur. If you read widely or intensively in a particular field, think about what you read, discuss it with your family and friends, you are learning. Or you may be learning on a more formal basis by taking a correspondence course, a television or radio course, a course recorded on tape or cassettes, a course assembled into programmed tests, or a course taught in your community adult school or high school.

No matter how, where, or when you gained your knowledge, you may have the opportunity to receive academic credit for your achievement that can be counted toward an undergraduate degree. The College-Level Examination Program (CLEP) enables colleges to evaluate your achievement and give you credit. A wide range of college-level examinations are offered by CLEP to anyone who wishes to take them. Scores on the tests are reported to you and, if you wish, to a college, employer, or individual.

2. WHAT ARE THE PURPOSES OF THE COLLEGE-LEVEL EXAMINATION PROGRAM?

The basic purpose of the College-Level Examination Program is to enable individuals who have acquired their education in nontraditional ways to demonstrate their academic achievement. It is also intended for use by those in higher education, business, industry, government, and other fields who need a reliable method of assessing a person's educational level.

Recognizing that the real issue is not how a person has acquired his education but what education he has, the College Level Examination Program has been designed to serve a variety of purposes. The basic purpose, as listed above, is to enable those who have reached the college level of education in nontraditional ways to assess the level of their achievement and to use the test results in seeking college credit or placement.

In addition, scores on the tests can be used to validate educational experience obtained at a nonaccredited institution or through noncredit college courses.

Some colleges and universities may use the tests to measure the level of educational achievement of their students, and for various institutional research purposes.

Other colleges and universities may wish to use the tests in the admission, placement, and guidance of students who wish to transfer from one institution to another.

Businesses, industries, governmental agencies, and professional groups now accept the results of these tests as a basis for advancement, eligibility for further training, or professional or semi-professional certification.

Many people are interested in the examination simply to assess their own educational progress and attainment.

The college, university, business, industry, or government agency that adopts the tests in the College-Level Examination Program makes its own decision about how it will use and interpret the test scores. The College Board will provide the tests, score them, and report the results either to the individuals who took the tests or the college or agency that administered them. It does NOT, and cannot, award college credit, certify college equivalency, or make recommendations regarding the standards these institutions should establish for the use of the test results.

Therefore, if you are taking the tests to secure credit from an institution, you should FIRST ascertain whether the college or agency involved will accept the scores. Each institution determines which CLEP tests it will accept for credit and the amount of credit it will award. If you want to take tests for college credit, first call, write, or visit the college you wish to attend to inquire about its policy on CLEP scores, as well as its other admission requirements.

The services of the program are also available to people who have been requested to take the tests by an employer, a professional licensing agency, a certifying agency, or by other groups that recognize college equivalency on the basis of satisfactory CLEP scores. You may, of course, take the tests SOLELY for your own information. If you do, your scores will be reported only to you.

While neither CLEP nor the College Board can evaluate previous credentials or award college credit, you will receive, with your scores, basic information to help you interpret your performance on the tests you have taken.

3. WHAT ARE THE COLLEGE-LEVEL EXAMINATIONS?

In order to meet different kinds of curricular organization and testing needs at colleges and universities, the College-Level Examination Program offers 35 different subject tests falling under five separate general categories: Composition and Literature, Foreign Languages, History and Social Sciences, Science and Mathematics, and Business.

4. WHAT ARE THE SUBJECT EXAMINATIONS?

The 35 CLEP tests offered by the College Board are listed below:

COMPOSITION AND LITERATURE:
- American Literature
- Analyzing and Interpreting Literature
- English Composition
- English Composition with Essay
- English Literature
- Freshman College Composition
- Humanities

FOREIGN LANGUAGES
- French
- German
- Spanish

HISTORY AND SOCIAL SCIENCES
- American Government
- Introduction to Educational Psychology
- History of the United States I: Early Colonization to 1877
- History of the United States II: 1865 to the Present
- Human Growth and Development
- Principles of Macroeconomics
- Principles of Microeconomics
- Introductory Psychology
- Social Sciences and History
- Introductory Sociology
- Western Civilization I: Ancient Near East to 1648
- Western Civilization II: 1648 to the Present

SCIENCE AND MATHEMATICS
- College Algebra
- College Algebra-Trigonometry
- Biology
- Calculus
- Chemistry
- College Mathematics
- Natural Sciences
- Trigonometry
- Precalculus

BUSINESS
- Financial Accounting
- Introductory Business Law
- Information Systems and Computer Applications
- Principles of Management
- Principles of Marketing

CLEP Examinations cover material taught in courses that most students take as requirements in the first two years of college. A college usually grants the same amount of credit to students earning satisfactory scores on the CLEP examination as it grants to students successfully completing the equivalent course.

Many examinations are designed to correspond to one-semester courses; some, however, correspond to full-year or two-year courses.

Each exam is 90 minutes long and, except for English Composition with Essay, is made up primarily of multiple-choice questions. Some tests have several other types of questions besides multiple choice. To see a more detailed description of a particular CLEP exam, visit www.collegeboard.com/clep.

The English Composition with Essay exam is the only exam that includes a required essay. This essay is scored by college English faculty designated by CLEP and does not require an additional fee. However, other Composition and Literature tests offer optional essays, which some college and universities require and some do not. These essays are graded by faculty at the individual institutions that require them and require an additional $10 fee. Contact the particular institution to ask about essay requirements, and check with your test center for further details.

All 35 CLEP examinations are administered on computer. If you are unfamiliar with taking a test on a computer, consult the CLEP Sampler online at www.collegeboard.com/clep. The Sampler contains the same tutorials as the actual exams and helps familiarize you with navigation and how to answer different types of questions.

Points are not deducted for wrong or skipped answers – you receive one point for every correct answer. Therefore it is best that an answer is supplied for each exam question, whether it is a guess or not. The number of correct answers is then converted to a formula score. This formula, or "scaled," score is determined by a statistical process called *equating*, which adjusts for slight differences in difficulty between test forms and ensures that your score does not depend on the specific test form you took or how well others did on the same form. The scaled scores range from 20 to 80 – this is the number that will appear on your score report.

To ensure that you complete all questions in the time allotted, you would probably be wise to skip the more difficult or perplexing questions and return to them later. Although the multiple-choice items in these tests are carefully designed so as not to be tricky, misleading, or ambiguous, on the other hand, they are not all direct questions of factual information. They attempt, in their way, to elicit a response that indicates your knowledge or lack of knowledge of the material in question or your ability or inability to use or interpret a fact or idea. Thus, you should concentrate on answering the questions as they appear to be without attempting to out-guess the testmakers.

5. WHAT ARE THE FEES?

The fee for all CLEP examinations is $55. Optional essays required by some institutions are an additional $10.

6. WHEN ARE THE TESTS GIVEN?

CLEP tests are administered year-round. Consult the CLEP website (www.collegeboard.com/clep) and individual test centers for specific information.

7. WHERE ARE THE TESTS GIVEN?

More than 1,300 test centers are located on college and university campuses throughout the country, and additional centers are being established to meet increased needs. Any accredited collegiate institution with an explicit and publicly available policy of credit by examination can become a CLEP test center. To obtain a list of these centers, visit the CLEP website at www.collegeboard.com/clep.

8. HOW DO I REGISTER FOR THE COLLEGE-LEVEL EXAMINATION PROGRAM?

Contact an individual test center for information regarding registration, scheduling and fees. Registration/admission forms can also be obtained on the CLEP website.

9. MAY I REPEAT THE COLLEGE-LEVEL EXAMINATIONS?

You may repeat any examination providing at least six months have passed since you were last administered this test. If you repeat a test within a period of time less than six months, your scores will be cancelled and your fees forfeited. To repeat a test, check the appropriate space on the registration form.

10. WHEN MAY I EXPECT MY SCORE REPORTS?

With the exception of the English Composition with Essay exam, you should receive your score report instantly once the test is complete.

11. HOW SHOULD I PREPARE FOR THE COLLEGE-LEVEL EXAMINATIONS?

This book has been specifically designed to prepare candidates for these examinations. It will help you to consider, study, and review important content, principles, practices, procedures, problems, and techniques in the form of varied and concrete applications.

12. QUESTIONS AND ANSWERS APPEARING IN THIS PUBLICATION

The College-Level Examinations are offered by the College Board. Since copies of past examinations have not been made available, we have used equivalent materials, including questions and answers, which are highly recommended by us as an appropriate means of preparing for these examinations.

If you need additional information about CLEP Examinations, visit www.collegeboard.com/clep.

THE COLLEGE-LEVEL EXAMINATION PROGRAM

How The Program Works

CLEP examinations are administered at many colleges and universities across the country, and most institutions award college credit to those who do well on them. The examinations provide people who have acquired knowledge outside the usual educational settings the opportunity to show that they have learned college-level material without taking certain college courses.

The CLEP examinations cover material that is taught in introductory-level courses at many colleges and universities. Faculties at individual colleges review the tests to ensure that they cover the important material taught in their courses. Colleges differ in the examinations they accept; some colleges accept only two or three of the examinations while others accept nearly all of them.

Although CLEP is sponsored by the College Board and the examinations are scored by Educational Testing Service (ETS), neither of these organizations can award college credit. Only accredited colleges may grant credit toward a degree. When you take a CLEP examination, you may request that a copy of your score report be sent to the college you are attending or plan to attend. After evaluating your scores, the college will decide whether or not to award you credit for a certain course or courses, or to exempt you from them. If the college gives you credit, it will record the number of credits on your permanent record, thereby indicating that you have completed work equivalent to a course in that subject. If the college decides to grant exemption without giving you credit for a course, you will be permitted to omit a course that would normally be required of you and to take a course of your choice instead.

What the Examinations Are Like

The examinations consist mostly of multiple-choice questions to be answered within a 90-minute time limit. Additional information about each CLEP examination is given in the examination guide and on the CLEP website.

<u>Where To Take the Examinations</u>

CLEP examinations are administered throughout the year at the test centers of approximately 1,300 colleges and universities. On the CLEP website, you will find a list of institutions that award credit for satisfactory scores on CLEP examinations. Some colleges administer CLEP examinations to their own students only. Other institutions administer the tests to anyone who registers to take them. If your college does not administer the tests, contact the test centers in your area for information about its testing schedule.

Once you have been tested, your score report will be available instantly. CLEP scores are kept on file at ETS for 20 years; and during this period, for a small fee, you may have your transcript sent to another college or to anyone else you specify. (Your scores will never be sent to anyone without your approval.)

APPROACHING A COLLEGE ABOUT CLEP

The following sections provide a step-by-step approach to learning about the CLEP policy at a particular college or university. The person or office that can best assist students desiring CLEP credit may have a different title at each institution, but the following guidelines will lead you to information about CLEP at any institution.

Adults returning to college often benefit from special assistance when they approach a college. Opportunities for adults to return to formal learning in the classroom are now widespread, and colleges and universities have worked hard to make this a smooth process for older students. Many colleges have established special service offices that are staffed with trained professionals who understand the kinds of problems facing adults returning to college. If you think you might benefit from such assistance, be sure to find out whether these services are available at your college.

<u>How to Apply for College Credit</u>

STEP 1. Obtain the General Information Catalog and a copy of the CLEP policy from the colleges you are considering. If you have not yet applied for admission, ask for an admissions application form too.

Information about admissions and CLEP policies can be obtained by contacting college admissions offices or finding admissions information on the school websites. Tell the admissions officer that you are a prospective student and that you are interested in applying for admission and CLEP credit. Ask for a copy of the publication in which the college's complete CLEP policy is explained. Also get the name and the telephone number of the person to contact in case you have further questions about CLEP.

At this step, you may wish to obtain information from external degree colleges. Many adults find that such colleges suit their needs exceptionally well.

STEP 2. If you have not already been admitted to the college you are considering, look at its admission requirements for undergraduate students to see if you can qualify.

This is an important step because if you can't get into college, you can't get college credit for CLEP. Nearly all colleges require students to be admitted and to enroll in one or more courses before granting the students CLEP credit.

Virtually all public community colleges and a number of four-year state colleges have open admission policies for in-state students. This usually means that they admit anyone who has graduated from high school or has earned a high school equivalency diploma.

If you think you do not meet the admission requirements, contact the admissions office for an interview with a counselor. Colleges do sometimes make exceptions, particularly for adult applicants. State why you want the interview and ask what documents you should bring with you or send in advance. (These materials may include a high school transcript, transcript of previous college work, completed application for admission, etc.) Make an extra effort to have all the information requested in time for the interview.

During the interview, relax and be yourself. Be prepared to state honestly why you think you are ready and able to do college work. If you have already taken CLEP examinations and scored high enough to earn credit, you have shown that you are able to do college work. Mention this achievement to the admissions counselor because it may increase your chances of being accepted. If you have not taken a CLEP examination, you can still improve your chances of being accepted by describing how your job training or independent study has helped prepare you for college-level work. Tell the counselor what you have learned from your work and personal experiences.

STEP 3. Evaluate the college's CLEP policy.

Typically, a college lists all its academic policies, including CLEP policies, in its general catalog. You will probably find the CLEP policy statement under a heading such as Credit-by-Examination, Advanced Standing, Advanced Placement, or External Degree Program. These sections can usually be found in the front of the catalog.

Many colleges publish their credit-by-examination policies in a separate brochure, which is distributed through the campus testing office, counseling center, admissions office, or registrar's office. If you find a very general policy statement in the college catalog, seek clarification from one of these offices.

Review the material in the section of this guide entitled Questions to Ask About a College's CLEP Policy. Use these guidelines to evaluate the college's CLEP policy. If you have not yet taken a CLEP examination, this evaluation will help you decide which examinations to take and whether or not to take the free-response or essay portion. Because individual colleges have different CLEP policies, a review of several policies may help you decide which college to attend.

STEP 4. If you have not yet applied for admission, do so early.

Most colleges expect you to apply for admission several months before you enroll, and it is essential that you meet the published application deadlines. It takes time to process your application for admission; and if you have yet to take a CLEP examination, it will be some time before the college receives and reviews your score report. You will probably want to take some, if not all, of the CLEP examinations you are interested in before you enroll so you know which courses you need not register for. In fact, some colleges require that all CLEP scores be submitted before a student registers.

Complete all forms and include all documents requested with your application(s) for admission. Normally, an admissions decision cannot be reached until all documents have been submitted and evaluated. Unless told to do so, do not send your CLEP scores until you have been officially admitted.

STEP 5. Arrange to take CLEP examination(s) or to submit your CLEP score(s).

You may want to wait to take your CLEP examinations until you know definitely which college you will be attending. Then you can make sure you are taking tests your college will accept for credit. You will also be able to request that your scores be sent to the college, free of charge, when you take the tests.

If you have already taken CLEP examinations, but did not have a copy of your score report sent to your college, you may request the College Board to send an official transcript at any time for a small fee. Use the Transcript Request Form that was sent to you with your score report. If you do not have the form, you may find it online at www.collegeboard.com/clep.

Your CLEP scores will be evaluated, probably by someone in the admissions office, and sent to the registrar's office to be posted on your permanent record once you are enrolled. Procedures vary from college to college, but the process usually begins in the admissions office.

STEP 6. Ask to receive a written notice of the credit you receive for your CLEP score(s).

A written notice may save you problems later, when you submit your degree plan or file for graduation. In the event that there is a question about whether or not you earned CLEP credit, you will have an official record of what credit was awarded. You may also need this verification of course credit if you go for academic counseling before the credit is posted on your permanent record.

STEP 7. Before you register for courses, seek academic counseling.

A discussion with your academic advisor can prevent you from taking unnecessary courses and can tell you specifically what your CLEP credit will mean to you. This step may be accomplished at the time you enroll. Most colleges have orientation sessions for new students prior to each enrollment period. During orientation, students are usually assigned an academic advisor who then gives them individual help in developing long-range plans and a course schedule for the next semester. In conjunction with this counseling, you may be asked to take some additional tests so that you can be placed at the proper course level.

External Degree Programs

If you have acquired a considerable amount of college-level knowledge through job experience, reading, or noncredit courses, if you have accumulated college credits at a variety of colleges over a period of years, or if you prefer studying on your own rather than in a classroom setting, you may want to investigate the possibility of enrolling in an external degree program. Many colleges offer external degree programs that allow you to earn a degree by passing examinations (including CLEP), transferring credit from other colleges, and demonstrating in other ways that you have satisfied the educational requirements. No classroom attendance is required, and the programs are open to out-of-state candidates as well as residents. Thomas A. Edison State College in New Jersey and Charter Oaks College in Connecticut are fully accredited independent state colleges; the New York program is part of the state university system and is also fully accredited. If you are interested in exploring an external degree, you can write for more information to:

Charter Oak College
The Exchange, Suite 171
270 Farmington Avenue
Farmington, CT 06032-1909

Regents External Degree Program
Cultural Education Center
Empire State Plaza
Albany, New York 12230

Thomas A. Edison State College
101 West State Street
Trenton, New Jersey 08608

Many other colleges also have external degree or weekend programs. While they often require that a number of courses be taken on campus, the external degree programs tend to be more flexible in transferring credit, granting credit-by-examination, and allowing independent study than other traditional programs. When applying to a college, you may wish to ask whether it has an external degree or weekend program.

Questions to Ask About a College's CLEP Policy

Before taking CLEP examinations for the purpose of earning college credit, try to find the answers to these questions:

1. Which CLEP examinations are accepted by this college?

A college may accept some CLEP examinations for credit and not others - possibly not the one you are considering. The English faculty may decide to grant college English credit based on the CLEP English Composition examination, but not on the Freshman College Composition examination. Or, the mathematics faculty may decide to grant credit based on the College Mathematics to non-mathematics majors only, requiring majors to take an examination in algebra, trigonometry, or calculus to earn credit. For these reasons, it is important that you know the specific CLEP tests for which you can receive credit.

2. Does the college require the optional free-response (essay) section as well as the objective portion of the CLEP examination you are considering?

Knowing the answer to this question ahead of time will permit you to schedule the optional essay examination when you register to take your CLEP examination.

3. Is credit granted for specific courses? If so, which ones?

You are likely to find that credit will be granted for specific courses and the course titles will be designated in the college's CLEP policy. It is not necessary, however, that credit be granted for a specific course in order for you to benefit from your CLEP credit. For instance, at many liberal arts colleges, all students must take certain types of courses; these courses may be labeled the core curriculum, general education requirements, distribution requirements, or liberal arts requirements. The requirements are often expressed in terms of credit hours. For example, all students may be required to take at least six hours of humanities, six hours of English, three hours of mathematics, six hours of natural science, and six hours of social science, with no particular courses in these disciplines specified. In these instances, CLEP credit may be given as 6 hrs. English credit or 3 hrs. Math credit without specifying for which English or mathematics courses credit has been awarded. In order to avoid possible disappointment, you should know before taking a CLEP examination what type of credit you can receive and whether you will only be exempted from a required course but receive no credit.

4. How much credit is granted for each examination you are considering, and does the college place a limit on the total amount of CLEP credit you can earn toward your degree?

Not all colleges that grant CLEP credit award the same amount for individual tests. Furthermore, some colleges place a limit on the total amount of credit you can earn through CLEP or other examinations. Other colleges may grant you exemption but no credit toward your degree. Knowing several colleges' policies concerning these issues may help you decide which college you will attend. If you think you are capable of passing a number of CLEP examinations, you may want to attend a college that will allow you to earn credit for all or most of them. For example, the state external degree programs grant credit for most CLEP examinations (and other tests as well).

5. What is the required score for earning CLEP credit for each test you are considering?

Most colleges publish the required scores or percentile ranks for earning CLEP credit in their general catalog or in a brochure. The required score may vary from test to test, so find out the required score for each test you are considering.

6. What is the college's policy regarding prior course work in the subject in which you are considering taking a CLEP test?

Some colleges will not grant credit for a CLEP test if the student has already attempted a college-level course closely aligned with that test. For example, if you successfully completed English 101 or a comparable course on another campus, you will probably not be permitted to receive CLEP credit in that subject, too. Some colleges will not permit you to earn CLEP credit for a course that you failed.

7. Does the college make additional stipulations before credit will be granted?

It is common practice for colleges to award CLEP credit only to their enrolled students. There are other stipulations, however, that vary from college to college. For example, does the college require you to formally apply for or accept CLEP credit by completing and signing a form? Or does the college require you to validate your CLEP score by successfully completing a more advanced course in the subject? Answers to these and other questions will help to smooth the process of earning college credit through CLEP.

The above questions and the discussions that follow them indicate some of the ways in which colleges' CLEP policies can vary. Find out as much as possible about the CLEP policies at the colleges you are interested in so you can choose a college with a policy that is compatible with your educational goals. Once you have selected the college you will attend, you can find out which CLEP examinations your college recognizes and the requirements for earning CLEP credit.

DECIDING WHICH EXAMINATIONS TO TAKE

If You're Taking the Examinations for College Credit or Career Advancement:

Most people who take CLEP examinations do so in order to earn credit for college courses. Others take the examinations in order to qualify for job promotions or for professional certification or licensing. It is vital to most candidates who are taking the tests for any of these reasons that they be well prepared for the tests they are taking so that they can advance as rapidly as possible toward their educational or career goals.

It is usually advisable that those who have limited knowledge in the subjects covered by the tests they are considering enroll in the college courses in which that material is taught. Those who are uncertain about whether or not they know enough about a subject to do well on a particular CLEP test will find the following guidelines helpful.

There is no way to predict if you will pass a particular CLEP examination, but answers to the questions under the seven headings below should give you an indication of whether or not you are likely to succeed.

1. Test Descriptions

Read the description of the test provided. Are you familiar with most of the topics and terminology in the outline?

2. Textbooks

Examine the suggested textbooks and other resource materials following the test descriptions in this guide. Have you recently read one or more of these books, or have you read similar college-level books on this subject? If you have not, read through one or more of the textbooks listed, or through the textbook used for this course at your college. Are you familiar with most of the topics and terminology in the book?

3. Sample Questions

The sample questions provided are intended to be typical of the content and difficulty of the questions on the test. Although they are not an exact miniature of the test, the proportion of the sample questions you can answer correctly should be a rough estimate of the proportion of questions you will be able to answer correctly on the test.

Answer as many of the sample questions for this test as you can. Check your answers against the correct answers. Did you answer more than half the questions correctly?

Because of variations in course content at different institutions, and because questions on CLEP tests vary from easy to difficult - with most being of moderate difficulty - the average student who passes a course in a subject can usually answer correctly about half the questions on the corresponding CLEP examination. Most colleges set their passing scores near this level, but some set them higher. If your college has set its required score above the level required by most colleges, you may need to answer a larger proportion of questions on the test correctly.

4. Previous Study

Have you taken noncredit courses in this subject offered by an adult school or a private school, through correspondence, or in connection with your job? Did you do exceptionally well in this subject in high school, or did you take an honors course in this subject?

5. Experience

Have you learned or used the knowledge or skills included in this test in your job or life experience? For example, if you lived in a Spanish-speaking country and spoke the language for a year or more, you might consider taking the Spanish examination. Or, if you have worked at a job in which you used accounting and finance skills, Principles of Accounting would be a likely test for you to take. Or, if you have read a considerable amount of literature and attended many art exhibits, concerts, and plays, you might expect to do well on the Humanities exam.

6. Other Examinations

Have you done well on other standardized tests in subjects related to the one you want to take? For example, did you score well above average on a portion of a college entrance examination covering similar skills, or did you obtain an exceptionally high score on a high school equivalency test or a licensing examination in this subject? Although such tests do not cover exactly the same material as the CLEP examinations and may be easier, persons who do well on these tests often do well on CLEP examinations, too.

7. Advice

Has a college counselor, professor, or some other professional person familiar with your ability advised you to take a CLEP examination?

If your answer was yes to questions under several of the above headings, you probably have a good chance of passing the CLEP examination you are considering. It is unlikely that you would have acquired sufficient background from experience alone. Learning gained through reading and study is essential, and you will probably find some additional study helpful before taking a CLEP examination.

If You're Taking the Examinations to Prepare for College

Many people entering college, particularly adults returning to college after several years away from formal education, are uncertain about their ability to compete with other college students. They wonder whether they have sufficient background for college study, and those who have been away from formal study for some time wonder whether they have forgotten how to study, how to take tests, and how to write papers. Such people may wish to improve their test-taking and study skills prior to enrolling in courses.

One way to assess your ability to perform at the college level and to improve your test-taking and study skills at the same time is to prepare for and take one or more CLEP examinations. You need not be enrolled in a college to take a CLEP examination, and you may have your scores sent only to yourself and later request that a transcript be sent to a college if you then decide to apply for credit. By reviewing the test descriptions and sample questions, you may find one or several subject areas in which you think you have substantial knowledge. Select one examination, or more if you like, and carefully read at least one of the textbooks listed in the bibliography for the test. By doing this, you will get a better idea of how much you know of what is usually taught in a college-level course in that subject. Study as much material as you can, until you think you have a good grasp of the subject matter. Then take the test at a college in your area. It will be several weeks before you receive your results, and you may wish to begin reviewing for another test in the meantime.

To find out if you are eligible for credit for your CLEP score, you must compare your score with the score required by the college you plan to attend. If you are not yet sure which college you will attend, or whether you will enroll in college at all, you should begin to follow the steps outlined. It is best that you do this before taking a CLEP test, but if you are taking the test only for the experience and to familiarize yourself with college-level material and requirements, you might take the test before you approach a college. Even if the college you decide to attend does not accept the test you took, the experience of taking such a test will enable you to meet with greater confidence the requirements of courses you will take.

You will find information about how to interpret your scores in WHAT YOUR SCORES MEAN, which you will receive with your score report, and which can also be found online at the CLEP website. Many colleges follow the recommendations of the American Council on Education (ACE) for setting their required scores, so you can use this information as a guide in determining how well you did. The ACE recommendations are included in the booklet.

If you do not do well enough on the test to earn college credit, don't be discouraged. Usually, it is the best college students who are exempted from courses or receive credit-by-examination. The fact that you cannot get credit for your score means that you should probably enroll in a college course to learn the material. However, if your score was close to the required score, or if you feel you could do better on a second try or after some additional study, you may retake the test after six months. Do not take it sooner or your score will not be reported and your fee will be forfeited.

If you do earn the score required to earn credit, you will have demonstrated that you already have some college-level knowledge. You will also have a better idea whether you should take additional CLEP examinations. And, what is most important, you can enroll in college with confidence, knowing that you do have the ability to succeed.

PREPARING TO TAKE CLEP EXAMINATIONS

Having made the decision to take one or more CLEP examinations, most people then want to know if it is worthwhile to prepare for them - how much, how long, when, and how should they go about it? The precise answers to these questions vary greatly from individual to individual. However, most candidates find that some type of test preparation is helpful.

Most people who take CLEP examinations do so to show that they have already learned the important material that is taught in a college course. Many of them need only a quick review to assure themselves that they have not forgotten some of what they once studied, and to fill in some of the gaps in their knowledge of the subject. Others feel that they need a thorough review and spend several weeks studying for a test. A few wish to take a CLEP examination as a kind of final examination for independent study of a subject instead of the college course. This last group requires significantly more study than those who only need to review, and they may need some guidance from professors of the subjects they are studying.

The key to how you prepare for CLEP examinations often lies in locating those skills and areas of prior learning in which you are strong and deciding where to focus your energies. Some people may know a great deal about a certain subject area, but may not test well. These individuals would probably be just as concerned about strengthening their test-taking skills as they are about studying for a specific test. Many mental and physical skills are used in preparing for a test. It is important not only to review or study for the examinations, but to make certain that you are alert, relatively free of anxiety, and aware of how to approach standardized tests. Suggestions on developing test-taking skills and preparing psychologically and physically for a test are given. The following section suggests ways of assessing your knowledge of the content of a test and then reviewing and studying the material.

Using This Study Guide

Begin by carefully reading the test description and outline of knowledge and skills required for the examination, if given. As you read through the topics listed there, ask yourself how much you know about each one. Also note the terms, names, and symbols that are mentioned, and ask yourself whether you are familiar with them. This will give you a quick overview of how much you know about the subject. If you are familiar with nearly all the material, you will probably need a minimum of review; however, if less than half of it is familiar, you will probably require substantial study to do well on the test.

If, after reviewing the test description, you find that you need extensive review, delay answering the sample question until you have done some reading in the subject. If you complete them before reviewing the material, you will probably look for the answers as you study, and then they will not be a good assessment of your ability at a later date.

If you think you are familiar with most of the test material, try to answer the sample questions.

Apply the test-taking strategies given. Keeping within the time limit suggested will give you a rough idea of how quickly you should work in order to complete the actual test.

Check your answers against the answer key. If you answered nearly all the questions correctly, you probably do not need to study the subject extensively. If you got about half the questions correct, you ought o review at least one textbook or other suggested materials on the subject. If you answered less than half the questions correctly, you will probably benefit from more extensive reading in the subject and thorough study of one or more textbooks. The textbooks listed are used at many colleges but they are not the only good texts. You will find helpful almost any standard text available to you., such as the textbook used at your college, or earlier editions of texts listed. For some examinations, topic outlines and textbooks may not be available. Take the sample tests in this book and check your answers at the end of each test. Check wrong answers.

Suggestions for Studying

The following suggestions have been gathered from people who have prepared for CLEP examinations or other college-level tests.

1. Define your goals and locate study materials

First, determine your study goals. Set aside a block of time to review the material provided in this book, and then decide which test(s) you will take. Using the suggestions, locate suitable resource materials. If a preparation course is offered by an adult school or college in your area, you might find it helpful to enroll.

2. Find a good place to study

To determine what kind of place you need for studying, ask yourself questions such as: Do I need a quiet place? Does the telephone distract me? Do objects I see in this place remind me of things I should do? Is it too warm? Is it well lit? Am I too comfortable here? Do I have space to spread out my materials? You may find the library more conducive to studying than your home. If you decide to study at home, you might prevent interruptions by other household members by putting a sign on the door of your study room to indicate when you will be available.

3. Schedule time to study

To help you determine where studying best fits into your schedule, try this exercise: Make a list of your daily activities (for example, sleeping, working, and eating) and estimate how many hours per day you spend on each activity. Now, rate all the activities on your list in order of their importance and evaluate your use of time. Often people are astonished at how an average day appears from this perspective. They may discover that they were unaware how large portions of time are spent, or they learn their time can be scheduled in alternative ways. For example, they can remove the least important activities from their day and devote that time to studying or another important activity.

4. Establish a study routine and a set of goals

In order to study effectively, you should establish specific goals and a schedule for accomplishing them. Some people find it helpful to write out a weekly schedule and cross out each study period when it is completed. Others maintain their concentration better by writing down the time when they expect to complete a study task. Most people find short periods of intense study more productive than long stretches of time. For example, they may follow a regular schedule of several 20- or 30-minute study periods with short breaks between them. Some people like to allow themselves rewards as they complete each study goal. It is not essential that you accomplish every goal exactly within your schedule; the point is to be committed to your task.

5. Learn how to take an active role in studying.

If you have not done much studying for some time, you may find it difficult to concentrate at first. Try a method of studying, such as the one outlined below, that will help you concentrate on and remember what you read.

    a. First, read the chapter summary and the introduction. Then you will know what to look for in your reading.

    b. Next, convert the section or paragraph headlines into questions. For example, if you are reading a section entitled, The Causes of the American Revolution, ask yourself: *What were the causes of the American Revolution?* Compose the answer as you read the paragraph. Reading and answering questions aloud will help you understand and remember the material.

c. Take notes on key ideas or concepts as you read. Writing will also help you fix concepts more firmly in your mind. Underlining key ideas or writing notes in your book can be helpful and will be useful for review. Underline only important points. If you underline more than a third of each paragraph, you are probably underlining too much.

d. If there are questions or problems at the end of a chapter, answer or solve them on paper as if you were asked to do them for homework. Mathematics textbooks (and some other books) sometimes include answers to some or all of the exercises. If you have such a book, write your answers before looking at the ones given. When problem-solving is involved, work enough problems to master the required methods and concepts. If you have difficulty with problems, review any sample problems or explanations in the chapter.

e. To retain knowledge, most people have to review the material periodically. If you are preparing for a test over an extended period of time, review key concepts and notes each week or so. Do not wait for weeks to review the material or you will need to relearn much of it.

Psychological and Physical Preparation

Most people feel at least some nervousness before taking a test. Adults who are returning to college may not have taken a test in many years or they may have had little experience with standardized tests. Some younger students, as well, are uncomfortable with testing situations. People who received their education in countries outside the United States may find that many tests given in this country are quite different from the ones they are accustomed to taking.

Not only might candidates find the types of tests and the kinds of questions on them unfamiliar, but other aspects of the testing environment may be strange as well. The physical and mental stress that results from meeting this new experience can hinder a candidate's ability to demonstrate his or her true degree of knowledge in the subject area being tested. For this reason, it is important to go to the test center well prepared, both mentally and physically, for taking the test. You may find the following suggestions helpful.

1. Familiarize yourself, as much as possible, with the test and the test situation before the day of the examination. It will be helpful for you to know ahead of time:

a. How much time will be allowed for the test and whether there are timed subsections.

b. What types of questions and directions appear on the examination.

c. How your test score will be computed.

d. How to properly answer the questions on the computer (See the CLEP Sample on the CLEP website)

e. In which building and room the examination will be administered. If you don't know where the building is, locate it or get directions ahead of time.

f. The time of the test administration. You might wish to confirm this information a day or two before the examination and find out what time the building and room will be open so that you can plan to arrive early.

g. Where to park your car or, if you wish to take public transportation, which bus or train to take and the location of the nearest stop.

h. Whether smoking will be permitted during the test.

i. Whether there will be a break between examinations (if you will be taking more than one on the same day), and whether there is a place nearby where you can get something to eat or drink.

2. Go to the test situation relaxed and alert. In order to prepare for the test:

a. Get a good night's sleep. Last minute cramming, particularly late the night before, is usually counterproductive.

b. Eat normally. It is usually not wise to skip breakfast or lunch on the day of the test or to eat a big meal just before the test.

c. Avoid tranquilizers and stimulants. If you follow the other directions in this book, you won't need artificial aids. It's better to be a little tense than to be drowsy, but stimulants such as coffee and cola can make you nervous and interfere with your concentration.

d. Don't drink a lot of liquids before the test. Having to leave the room during the test will disturb your concentration and take valuable time away from the test.

e. If you are inclined to be nervous or tense, learn some relaxation exercises and use them before and perhaps during the test.

3. Arrive for the test early and prepared. Be sure to:

a. Arrive early enough so that you can find a parking place, locate the test center, and get settled comfortably before testing begins. Allow some extra time in case you are delayed unexpectedly.

b. Take the following with you:

- Your completed Registration/Admission Form
- Two forms of identification – one being a government-issued photo ID with signature, such as a driver's license or passport
- Non-mechanical pencil
- A watch so that you can time your progress (digital watches are prohibited)
- Your glasses if you need them for reading or seeing the chalkboard or wall clock

c. Leave all books, papers, and notes outside the test center. You will not be permitted to use your own scratch paper; it will be provided. Also prohibited are calculators, cell phones, beepers, pagers, photo/copy devices, radios, headphones, food, beverages, and several other items.

d. Be prepared for any temperature in the testing room. Wear layers of clothing that can be removed if the room is too hot but will keep you warm if it is too cold.

4. When you enter the test room:

a. Sit in a seat that provides a maximum of comfort and freedom from distraction.

b. Read directions carefully, and listen to all instructions given by the test administrator. If you don't understand the directions, ask for help before test timing begins. If you must ask a question after the test has begun, raise your hand and a proctor will assist you. The proctor can answer certain kinds of questions but cannot help you with the test.

c. Know your rights as a test taker. You can expect to be given the full working time allowed for the test(s) and a reasonably quiet and comfortable place in which to work. If a poor test situation is preventing you from doing your best, ask if the situation can be remedied. If bad test conditions cannot be remedied, ask the person in charge to report the problem in the Irregularity Report that will be sent to ETS with the answer sheets. You may also wish to contact CLEP. Describe the exact circumstances as completely as you can. Be sure to include the test date and name(s) of the test(s) you took. ETS will investigate the problem to make sure it does not happen again, and, if the problem is serious enough, may arrange for you to retake the test without charge.

TAKING THE EXAMINATIONS

A person may know a great deal about the subject being tested, but not do as well as he or she is capable of on the test. Knowing how to approach a test is an important part of the testing process. While a command of test-taking skills cannot substitute for knowledge of the subject matter, it can be a significant factor in successful testing.

Test-taking skills enable a person to use all available information to earn a score that truly reflects his or her ability. There are different strategies for approaching different kinds of test questions. For example, free-response questions require a very different tack than do multiple-choice questions. Other factors, such as how the test will be graded, may also influence your approach to the test and your use of test time. Thus, your preparation for a test should include finding out all you can about the test so that you can use the most effective test-taking strategies.

Before taking a test, you should know approximately how many questions are on the test, how much time you will be allowed, how the test will be scored or graded, what types of questions and directions are on the test, and how you will be required to record your answers.

Taking Multiple-Choice Tests

1. Listen carefully to the instructions given by the test administrator and read carefully all directions before you begin to answer the questions.

2. Note the time that the test administrator starts timing the test. As you proceed, make sure that you are not working too slowly. You should have answered at least half the questions in a section when half the time for that section has passed. If you have not reached that point in the section, speed up your pace on the remaining questions.

3. Before answering a question, read the entire question, including all the answer choices. Don't think that because the first or second answer choice looks good to you, it isn't necessary to read the remaining options. Instructions usually tell you to select the best answer. Sometimes one answer choice is partially correct, but another option is better; therefore, it is usually a good idea to read all the answers before you choose one.

4. Read and consider every question. Questions that look complicated at first glance may not actually be so difficult once you have read them carefully.

5. Do not puzzle too long over any one question. If you don't know the answer after you've considered it briefly, go on to the next question. Make sure you return to the question later.

6. Make sure you record your response properly.

7. In trying to determine the correct answer, you may find it helpful to cross out those options that you know are incorrect, and to make marks next to those you think might be correct. If you decide to skip the question and come back to it later, you will save yourself the time of reconsidering all the options.

8. Watch for the following key words in test questions:

all	generally	never	perhaps
always	however	none	rarely
but	may	not	seldom
except	must	often	sometimes
every	necessary	only	usually

When a question or answer option contains words such as always, every, only, never, and none, there can be no exceptions to the answer you choose. Use of words such as often, rarely, sometimes, and generally indicates that there may be some exceptions to the answer.

9. Do not waste your time looking for clues to right answers based on flaws in question wording or patterns in correct answers. Professionals at the College Board and ETS put

a great deal of effort into developing valid, reliable, fair tests. CLEP test development committees are composed of college faculty who are experts in the subject covered by the test and are appointed by the College Board to write test questions and to scrutinize each question that is included on a CLEP test. Committee members make every effort to ensure that the questions are not ambiguous, that they have only one correct answer, and that they cover college-level topics. These committees do not intentionally include trick questions. If you think a question is flawed, ask the test administrator to report it, or contact CLEP immediately.

Taking Free-Response or Essay Tests

If your college requires the optional free-response or essay portion of a CLEP Composition and Literature exams, you should do some additional preparation for your CLEP test. Taking an essay test is very different from taking a multiple-choice test, so you will need to use some other strategies.

The essay written as part of the English Composition and Essay exam is graded by English professors from a variety of colleges and universities. A process called holistic scoring is used to rate your writing ability.

The optional free-response essays, on the other hand, are graded by the faculty of the college you designate as a score recipient. Guidelines and criteria for grading essays are not specified by the College Board or ETS. You may find it helpful, therefore, to talk with someone at your college to find out what criteria will be used to determine whether you will get credit. If the test requires essay responses, ask how much emphasis will be placed on your writing ability and your ability to organize your thoughts as opposed to your knowledge of subject matter. Find out how much weight will be given to your multiple-choice test score in comparison with your free-response grade in determining whether you will get credit. This will give you an idea where you should expend the greatest effort in preparing for and taking the test.

Here are some strategies you will find useful in taking any essay test:

1. Before you begin to write, read all questions carefully and take a few minutes to jot down some ideas you might include in each answer.

2. If you are given a choice of questions to answer, choose the questions you think you can answer most clearly and knowledgeably.

3. Determine in what order you will answer the questions. Answer those you find the easiest first so that any extra time can be spent on the more difficult questions.

4. When you know which questions you will answer and in what order, determine how much testing time remains and estimate how many minutes you will devote to each question. Unless suggested times are given for the questions or one question appears to require more or less time than the others, allot an equal amount of time to each question.

5. Before answering each question, indicate the number of the question as it is given in the test book. You need not copy the entire question from the question sheet, but it will be helpful to you and to the person grading your test if you indicate briefly the topic you are addressing – particularly if you are not answering the questions in the order in which they appear on the test.

6. Before answering each question, read it again carefully to make sure you are interpreting it correctly. Underline key words, such as those listed below, that often appear in free-response questions. Be sure you know the exact meaning of these words before taking the test.

analyze	demonstrate	enumerate	list
apply	derive	explain	outline
assess	describe	generalize	prove
compare	determine	illustrate	rank
contrast	discuss	interpret	show
define	distinguish	justify	summarize

If a question asks you to outline, define, or summarize, do not write a detailed explanation; if a question asks you to analyze, explain, illustrate, interpret, or show, you must do more than briefly describe the topic.

For a current listing of CLEP Colleges

where you can get credit and be tested, write:

CLEP, P.O. Box 6600, Princeton, NJ 08541-6600

Or e-mail: clep@ets.org, or call: (609) 771-7865

INFORMATION SYSTEMS

Description of the Examination

The Information Systems examination covers material that is usually taught in an introductory college-level business information systems course. Questions test knowledge, terminology, and basic concepts about information systems as well as the application of that knowledge. The examination does not emphasize the details of hardware design and language-specific programming techniques. References to applications such as word processing or spreadsheets do not require knowledge of a specific product. The focus is on concepts and techniques applicable to a variety of products and environments. Knowledge of arithmetic and mathematics equivalent to that of a student who has successfully completed a traditional first-year high school algebra course is assumed.

The examination contains approximately 100 questions to be answered in 90 minutes. Some of these are pretest questions and will not be scored. The time candidates spend on tutorials and providing personal information is in addition to the actual testing time.

Knowledge and Skills Required

Questions on the Information Systems examination require candidates to demonstrate knowledge of the following content. The percentages next to each main topic indicate the approximate percentage of exam questions on that topic.

10%   Office Applications
- Productivity software(word processing, spreadsheet, presentation package, end-user database package)
- Operating systems (memory management, file management, interfaces, types of OS)
- Office systems (e-mail, conferencing, collaborative work, document imaging, system resources)

15%   Internet and World Wide Web
- Internet and other online services and methods (World Wide Web, protocol, Web search engines, Web bots, intranet, cloud computing, communications, push/pull technology, W3C)
- Web browsers (URLs, protocols, standards, history, cookies, resource allocation)
- Web technologies (HTML, XML, Javascript)
- Website development (analysis, design, functionality, accessibility)

15%   Technology Applications
- Specialized systems (knowledge management, expert systems, TPS/OLTP, DSS, GIS, BI, workflow management, project management)
- E-commerce/E-business (EDI, standards, tools, characteristics, types of transactions, business models)
- Enterprise-wide systems (ERP, CRM, SCM)
- Data management (data warehousing, data mining, networking, security, validation, migration, storage, obsolescence)
- Business strategies (competition, process re-engineering, process modeling, TQM, Web 2.0)
- Information processing methods (batch, real-time, transaction)

15%   Hardware and Systems Technology

- Devices (processing, storage, input and output, telecommunications, networking)
- Functions (computer, telecommunications, network hardware)
- Network architectures (local area, wide area, VPN, enterprise)
- Computer architectures (mainframe, client/server, operating systems)
- Wireless technologies (Wi-Fi, cellular, satellite, mobile, GPS, RFID)

10%   Software Development

- Methodologies (prototyping, SDLC, RAD, CASE, JAD, Agile)
- Processes (feasibility, systems analysis, systems design, end-user development, project management)
- Implementation (testing, training, data conversion, system conversion, system maintenance, post-implementation activities, post-implementation review, documentation)
- Standards (proprietary, open source)
- User interface design
- Development and purpose of standards

10%   Programming Concepts and Data Management

- Programming logic (Boolean, arithmetic, SQL)
- Methodologies (object-oriented, structured)
- Data (concepts, types, structures, digital representation of data)
- File (types, structures)
- Database management systems (relational, hierarchical, network, management strategies)

25%   Social and Ethical Implications and Issues

- Economic effects (secure transactions, viruses, malware, cost of security)
- Privacy concerns (individual, business, identity theft)
- Property rights (intellectual, legal, ownership of materials, open-source software)
- Effects of information technology on jobs (ergonomics, virtual teams, telecommuting, job design)
- Technology's influence on workforce strategies (globalization, virtual teams, telecommuting, outsourcing, insourcing)
- Careers in IS (responsibilities, occupations, career path, certification)
- Computer security and controls (system application, personal computer, disaster recovery)
- Social networking (benefits, risks, ethics, technology, Web 2.0

HOW TO TAKE A TEST

You have studied long, hard and conscientiously.

With your official admission card in hand, and your heart pounding, you have been admitted to the examination room.

You note that there are several hundred other applicants in the examination room waiting to take the same test.

They all appear to be equally well prepared.

You know that nothing but your best effort will suffice. The "moment of truth" is at hand: you now have to demonstrate objectively, in writing, your knowledge of content and your understanding of subject matter.

You are fighting the most important battle of your life—to pass and/or score high on an examination which will determine your career and provide the economic basis for your livelihood.

What extra, special things should you know and should you do in taking the examination?

I. YOU MUST PASS AN EXAMINATION

A. WHAT EVERY CANDIDATE SHOULD KNOW
Examination applicants often ask us for help in preparing for the written test. What can I study in advance? What kinds of questions will be asked? How will the test be given? How will the papers be graded?

B. HOW ARE EXAMS DEVELOPED?
Examinations are carefully written by trained technicians who are specialists in the field known as "psychological measurement," in consultation with recognized authorities in the field of work that the test will cover. These experts recommend the subject matter areas or skills to be tested; only those knowledges or skills important to your success on the job are included. The most reliable books and source materials available are used as references. Together, the experts and technicians judge the difficulty level of the questions.

Test technicians know how to phrase questions so that the problem is clearly stated. Their ethics do not permit "trick" or "catch" questions. Questions may have been tried out on sample groups, or subjected to statistical analysis, to determine their usefulness.

Written tests are often used in combination with performance tests, ratings of training and experience, and oral interviews. All of these measures combine to form the best-known means of finding the right person for the right job.

II. HOW TO PASS THE WRITTEN TEST

A. BASIC STEPS

1) Study the announcement

How, then, can you know what subjects to study? Our best answer is: "Learn as much as possible about the class of positions for which you've applied." The exam will test the knowledge, skills and abilities needed to do the work.

Your most valuable source of information about the position you want is the official exam announcement. This announcement lists the training and experience qualifications. Check these standards and apply only if you come reasonably close to meeting them. Many jurisdictions preview the written test in the exam announcement by including a section called "Knowledge and Abilities Required," "Scope of the Examination," or some similar heading. Here you will find out specifically what fields will be tested.

2) Choose appropriate study materials

If the position for which you are applying is technical or advanced, you will read more advanced, specialized material. If you are already familiar with the basic principles of your field, elementary textbooks would waste your time. Concentrate on advanced textbooks and technical periodicals. Think through the concepts and review difficult problems in your field.

These are all general sources. You can get more ideas on your own initiative, following these leads. For example, training manuals and publications of the government agency which employs workers in your field can be useful, particularly for technical and professional positions. A letter or visit to the government department involved may result in more specific study suggestions, and certainly will provide you with a more definite idea of the exact nature of the position you are seeking.

3) Study this book!

III. KINDS OF TESTS

Tests are used for purposes other than measuring knowledge and ability to perform specified duties. For some positions, it is equally important to test ability to make adjustments to new situations or to profit from training. In others, basic mental abilities not dependent on information are essential. Questions which test these things may not appear as pertinent to the duties of the position as those which test for knowledge and information. Yet they are often highly important parts of a fair examination. For very general questions, it is almost impossible to help you direct your study efforts. What we can do is to point out some of the more common of these general abilities needed in public service positions and describe some typical questions.

1) General information

Broad, general information has been found useful for predicting job success in some kinds of work. This is tested in a variety of ways, from vocabulary lists to questions about current events. Basic background in some field of work, such as sociology or economics, may be sampled in a group of questions. Often these are principles which have become familiar to most persons through exposure rather than through formal training. It is difficult to advise you how to study for these questions; being alert to the world around you is our best suggestion.

2) Verbal ability

An example of an ability needed in many positions is verbal or language ability. Verbal ability is, in brief, the ability to use and understand words. Vocabulary and grammar tests are typical measures of this ability. Reading comprehension or paragraph interpretation questions are common in many kinds of civil service tests. You are given a paragraph of written material and asked to find its central meaning.

IV. KINDS OF QUESTIONS

1. Multiple-choice Questions

Most popular of the short-answer questions is the "multiple choice" or "best answer" question. It can be used, for example, to test for factual knowledge, ability to solve problems or judgment in meeting situations found at work.

A multiple-choice question is normally one of three types:

- It can begin with an incomplete statement followed by several possible endings. You are to find the one ending which *best* completes the statement, although some of the others may not be entirely wrong.
- It can also be a complete statement in the form of a question which is answered by choosing one of the statements listed.
- It can be in the form of a problem – again you select the best answer.

Here is an example of a multiple-choice question with a discussion which should give you some clues as to the method for choosing the right answer:

When an employee has a complaint about his assignment, the action which will *best* help him overcome his difficulty is to
A. discuss his difficulty with his coworkers
B. take the problem to the head of the organization
C. take the problem to the person who gave him the assignment
D. say nothing to anyone about his complaint

In answering this question, you should study each of the choices to find which is best. Consider choice "A" – Certainly an employee may discuss his complaint with fellow employees, but no change or improvement can result, and the complaint remains unresolved. Choice "B" is a poor choice since the head of the organization probably does not know what assignment you have been given, and taking your problem to him is known as "going over the head" of the supervisor. The supervisor, or person who made the assignment, is the person who can clarify it or correct any injustice. Choice "C" is, therefore, correct. To say nothing, as in choice "D," is unwise. Supervisors have and interest in knowing the problems employees are facing, and the employee is seeking a solution to his problem.

2. True/False

3. Matching Questions
Matching an answer from a column of choices within another column.

V. RECORDING YOUR ANSWERS

Computer terminals are used more and more today for many different kinds of exams.
For an examination with very few applicants, you may be told to record your answers in the test booklet itself. Separate answer sheets are much more common. If this separate answer sheet is to be scored by machine – and this is often the case – it is highly important that you mark your answers correctly in order to get credit.

VI. BEFORE THE TEST

YOUR PHYSICAL CONDITION IS IMPORTANT
If you are not well, you can't do your best work on tests. If you are half asleep, you can't do your best either. Here are some tips:

1) Get about the same amount of sleep you usually get. Don't stay up all night before the test, either partying or worrying—DON'T DO IT!
2) If you wear glasses, be sure to wear them when you go to take the test. This goes for hearing aids, too.
3) If you have any physical problems that may keep you from doing your best, be sure to tell the person giving the test. If you are sick or in poor health, you relay cannot do your best on any test. You can always come back and take the test some other time.

Common sense will help you find procedures to follow to get ready for an examination. Too many of us, however, overlook these sensible measures. Indeed, nervousness and fatigue have been found to be the most serious reasons why applicants fail to do their best on civil service tests. Here is a list of reminders:

• Begin your preparation early – Don't wait until the last minute to go scurrying around for books and materials or to find out what the position is all about.
• Prepare continuously – An hour a night for a week is better than an all-night cram session. This has been definitely established. What is more, a night a week for a month will return better dividends than crowding your study into a shorter period of time.
• Locate the place of the exam – You have been sent a notice telling you when and where to report for the examination. If the location is in a different town or otherwise unfamiliar to you, it would be well to inquire the best route and learn something about the building.
• Relax the night before the test – Allow your mind to rest. Do not study at all that night. Plan some mild recreation or diversion; then go to bed early and get a good night's sleep.
• Get up early enough to make a leisurely trip to the place for the test – This way unforeseen events, traffic snarls, unfamiliar buildings, etc. will not upset you.

- Dress comfortably – A written test is not a fashion show. You will be known by number and not by name, so wear something comfortable.
- Leave excess paraphernalia at home – Shopping bags and odd bundles will get in your way. You need bring only the items mentioned in the official notice you received; usually everything you need is provided. Do not bring reference books to the exam. They will only confuse those last minutes and be taken away from you when in the test room.
- Arrive somewhat ahead of time – If because of transportation schedules you must get there very early, bring a newspaper or magazine to take your mind off yourself while waiting.
- Locate the examination room – When you have found the proper room, you will be directed to the seat or part of the room where you will sit. Sometimes you are given a sheet of instructions to read while you are waiting. Do not fill out any forms until you are told to do so; just read them and be prepared.
- Relax and prepare to listen to the instructions
- If you have any physical problem that may keep you from doing your best, be sure to tell the test administrator. If you are sick or in poor health, you really cannot do your best on the exam. You can come back and take the test some other time.

VII. AT THE TEST

The day of the test is here and you have the test booklet in your hand. The temptation to get going is very strong. Caution! There is more to success than knowing the right answers. You must know how to identify your papers and understand variations in the type of short-answer question used in this particular examination. Follow these suggestions for maximum results from your efforts:

1) Cooperate with the monitor

The test administrator has a duty to create a situation in which you can be as much at ease as possible. He will give instructions, tell you when to begin, check to see that you are marking your answer sheet correctly, and so on. He is not there to guard you, although he will see that your competitors do not take unfair advantage. He wants to help you do your best.

2) Listen to all instructions

Don't jump the gun! Wait until you understand all directions. In most civil service tests you get more time than you need to answer the questions. So don't be in a hurry. Read each word of instructions until you clearly understand the meaning. Study the examples, listen to all announcements and follow directions. Ask questions if you do not understand what to do.

3) Identify your papers

Civil service exams are usually identified by number only. You will be assigned a number; you must not put your name on your test papers. Be sure to copy your number correctly. Since more than one exam may be given, copy your exact examination title.

4) Plan your time

Unless you are told that a test is a "speed" or "rate of work" test, speed itself is usually not important. Time enough to answer all the questions will be provided, but this does not mean that you have all day. An overall time limit has been set. Divide the total time (in minutes) by the number of questions to determine the approximate time you have for each question.

5) Do not linger over difficult questions

If you come across a difficult question, mark it with a paper clip (useful to have along) and come back to it when you have been through the booklet. One caution if you do this – be sure to skip a number on your answer sheet as well. Check often to be sure that you have not lost your place and that you are marking in the row numbered the same as the question you are answering.

6) Read the questions

Be sure you know what the question asks! Many capable people are unsuccessful because they failed to *read* the questions correctly.

7) Answer all questions

Unless you have been instructed that a penalty will be deducted for incorrect answers, it is better to guess than to omit a question.

8) Speed tests

It is often better NOT to guess on speed tests. It has been found that on timed tests people are tempted to spend the last few seconds before time is called in marking answers at random – without even reading them – in the hope of picking up a few extra points. To discourage this practice, the instructions may warn you that your score will be "corrected" for guessing. That is, a penalty will be applied. The incorrect answers will be deducted from the correct ones, or some other penalty formula will be used.

9) Review your answers

If you finish before time is called, go back to the questions you guessed or omitted to give them further thought. Review other answers if you have time.

10) Return your test materials

If you are ready to leave before others have finished or time is called, take ALL your materials to the monitor and leave quietly. Never take any test material with you. The monitor can discover whose papers are not complete, and taking a test booklet may be grounds for disqualification.

VIII. EXAMINATION TECHNIQUES

1) Read the general instructions carefully. These are usually printed on the first page of the exam booklet. As a rule, these instructions refer to the timing of the examination; the fact that you should not start work until the signal and must stop work at a signal, etc. If there are any *special* instructions, such as a choice of questions to be answered, make sure that you note this instruction carefully.

2) When you are ready to start work on the examination, that is as soon as the signal has been given, read the instructions to each question booklet, underline any key words or phrases, such as *least, best, outline, describe*

and the like. In this way you will tend to answer as requested rather than discover on reviewing your paper that you *listed without describing*, that you selected the *worst* choice rather than the *best* choice, etc.

3) If the examination is of the objective or multiple-choice type – that is, each question will also give a series of possible answers: A, B, C or D, and you are called upon to select the best answer and write the letter next to that answer on your answer paper – it is advisable to start answering each question in turn. There may be anywhere from 50 to 100 such questions in the three or four hours allotted and you can see how much time would be taken if you read through all the questions before beginning to answer any. Furthermore, if you come across a question or group of questions which you know would be difficult to answer, it would undoubtedly affect your handling of all the other questions.

4) If the examination is of the essay type and contains but a few questions, it is a moot point as to whether you should read all the questions before starting to answer any one. Of course, if you are given a choice – say five out of seven and the like – then it is essential to read all the questions so you can eliminate the two that are most difficult. If, however, you are asked to answer all the questions, there may be danger in trying to answer the easiest one first because you may find that you will spend too much time on it. The best technique is to answer the first question, then proceed to the second, etc.

5) Time your answers. Before the exam begins, write down the time it started, then add the time allowed for the examination and write down the time it must be completed, then divide the time available somewhat as follows:
   - If 3-1/2 hours are allowed, that would be 210 minutes. If you have 80 objective-type questions, that would be an average of 2-1/2 minutes per question. Allow yourself no more than 2 minutes per question, or a total of 160 minutes, which will permit about 50 minutes to review.
   - If for the time allotment of 210 minutes there are 7 essay questions to answer, that would average about 30 minutes a question. Give yourself only 25 minutes per question so that you have about 35 minutes to review.

6) The most important instruction is to *read each question* and make sure you know what is wanted. The second most important instruction is to *time yourself properly* so that you answer every question. The third most important instruction is to *answer every question*. Guess if you have to but include something for each question. Remember that you will receive no credit for a blank and will probably receive some credit if you write something in answer to an essay question. If you guess a letter – say "B" for a multiple-choice question – you may have guessed right. If you leave a blank as an answer to a multiple-choice question, the examiners may respect your feelings but it will not add a point to your score. Some exams may penalize you for wrong answers, so in such cases *only*, you may not want to guess unless you have some basis for your answer.

7) Suggestions
   a. Objective-type questions
      1. Examine the question booklet for proper sequence of pages and questions
      2. Read all instructions carefully
      3. Skip any question which seems too difficult; return to it after all other questions have been answered
      4. Apportion your time properly; do not spend too much time on any single question or group of questions
      5. Note and underline key words – *all, most, fewest, least, best, worst, same, opposite,* etc.
      6. Pay particular attention to negatives
      7. Note unusual option, e.g., unduly long, short, complex, different or similar in content to the body of the question
      8. Observe the use of "hedging" words – *probably, may, most likely,* etc.
      9. Make sure that your answer is put next to the same number as the question
      10. Do not second-guess unless you have good reason to believe the second answer is definitely more correct
      11. Cross out original answer if you decide another answer is more accurate; do not erase until you are ready to hand your paper in
      12. Answer all questions; guess unless instructed otherwise
      13. Leave time for review

   b. Essay questions
      1. Read each question carefully
      2. Determine exactly what is wanted. Underline key words or phrases.
      3. Decide on outline or paragraph answer
      4. Include many different points and elements unless asked to develop any one or two points or elements
      5. Show impartiality by giving pros and cons unless directed to select one side only
      6. Make and write down any assumptions you find necessary to answer the questions
      7. Watch your English, grammar, punctuation and choice of words
      8. Time your answers; don't crowd material

8) Answering the essay question

Most essay questions can be answered by framing the specific response around several key words or ideas. Here are a few such key words or ideas:

M's: manpower, materials, methods, money, management
P's: purpose, program, policy, plan, procedure, practice, problems, pitfalls, personnel, public relations
a. Six basic steps in handling problems:
   1. Preliminary plan and background development
   2. Collect information, data and facts
   3. Analyze and interpret information, data and facts
   4. Analyze and develop solutions as well as make recommendations

5. Prepare report and sell recommendations
6. Install recommendations and follow up effectiveness

b. Pitfalls to avoid
1. *Taking things for granted* – A statement of the situation does not necessarily imply that each of the elements is necessarily true; for example, a complaint may be invalid and biased so that all that can be taken for granted is that a complaint has been registered
2. *Considering only one side of a situation* – Wherever possible, indicate several alternatives and then point out the reasons you selected the best one
3. *Failing to indicate follow up* – Whenever your answer indicates action on your part, make certain that you will take proper follow-up action to see how successful your recommendations, procedures or actions turn out to be
4. *Taking too long in answering any single question* – Remember to time your answers properly

EXAMINATION SECTION

EXAMINATION SECTION

TEST 1

DIRECTIONS: Each question or incomplete statement is followed by several suggested answers or completions. Select the one that BEST answers the question or completes the statement. *PRINT THE LETTER OF THE CORRECT ANSWER IN THE SPACE AT THE RIGHT.*

1. Physical components of computers are known as
   A. software   B. hardware   C. firmware   D. human ware
   1. _B_

2. A touchscreen is considered a(n) _____ device.
   A. input   B. output   C. display   D. both A and B
   2. _D_

3. Keyboards and microphones are examples of computer
   A. peripherals   B. software   C. add-ons   D. uploads
   3. _A_

4. Unauthorized access to a computer is prevented through the use of
   A. passwords   B. user logins
   C. access control software   D. computer keys
   4. _A_

5. In order to establish an Internet connection, a modem is always connected to a
   A. keyboard   B. monitor
   C. telephone line   D. printer
   5. _C_

6. _____ does NOT hold data permanently.
   A. RAM   B. ROM   C. Hard drive   D. Flash drive
   6. _A_

7. Identification of a user who comes back to the same website is done through the use of
   A. scripts   B. plug-in   C. cookies   D. both A and B
   7. _C_

8. File _____ is the process of moving a file from one computer to another computer across the network.
   A. encryption   B. transfer   C. copying   D. updating
   8. _B_

9. _____ is a type of software that controls specific hardware.
   A. Driver   B. Browser   C. Plug-in   D. Control panel
   9. _A_

10. _____ is a downloadable program that is used for Internet surfing.
   A. Messenger   B. Firefox
   C. Windows Explorer   D. Internet
   10. _B_

11. In Microsoft Word, _____ is NOT a font style.
   A. Bold   B. Regular   C. Superscript   D. Italic
   11. _C_

1

12. Which of the following is NOT associated with page margins in a Word document?   12. _B_
   A. Top   B. Center   C. Left   D. Right

13. Microsoft Office is a type of _____ software.   13. _A_
   A. application   B. system   C. Internet   D. website

14. A function that is inside another function is known as a(n) _____ function.   14. _B_
   A. round   B. nested   C. sum   D. average

15. To write a formula in Microsoft Excel, a user would start by typing   15. _B_
   A. %   B. =   C. #   D. @

16. The individual boxes used for data entry in an Excel file are known as   16. _A_
   A. cells   B. data points
   C. formulas   D. squares

17. In PowerPoint, _____ do NOT show with the slide layout.   17. _B_
   A. titles   B. animations   C. lists   D. charts

18. _____ is a basic option when looking for colorful images or graphics to publish in a PowerPoint presentation.   18. _A_
   A. Clip art   B. Online search
   C. MS Paint   D. Drawing

19. In a web browser, the addresses of Internet pages are known as   19. _B_
   A. web pages   B. URLs   C. scripts   D. plug-in

20. A company that provides Internet services is called a(n)   20. _B_
   A. ISP   B. IBM   C. LAN   D. Both A and B

21. _____ is the process of copying a file from personal computer to a remote computer.   21. ____
   A. Downloading   B. Uploading
   C. Updating   D. Modification

22. _____ is a text that opens another page when clicked.   22. ____
   A. Link   B. Hyperlink
   C. Both A and B   D. Web page

23. Dots per inch is the measure of printing   23. _A_
   A. quality   B. type   C. time   D. layout

24. _____ is the collection of computers connected with each other.   24. _C_
   A. Group   B. Team   C. Network   D. Meeting

25. Which one of the following is considered a high-end printer?   25. _C_
   A. Dot matrix printer   B. Inkjet printer
   C. Laser   D. Thermal

KEY (CORRECT ANSWERS)

1.	B		11.	C
2.	D		12.	B
3.	A		13.	A
4.	A		14.	B
5.	C		15.	B
6.	A		16.	A
7.	C		17.	B
8.	B		18.	A
9.	A		19.	B
10.	B		20.	A

21.	B
22.	C
23.	A
24.	C
25.	C

TEST 2

DIRECTIONS: Each question or incomplete statement is followed by several suggested answers or completions. Select the one that BEST answers the question or completes the statement. *PRINT THE LETTER OF THE CORRECT ANSWER IN THE SPACE AT THE RIGHT.*

1. Which one of the following is a storage device?   1. _B_
   A. Printer   B. Hard drive
   C. Scanner   D. Motherboard

2. DVD is an example of a(n) _____ disk.   2. _B_
   A. hard   B. optical   C. magnetic   D. floppy

3. _____ computers provide resources to other computers across the network.   3. _A_
   A. Server   B. Client   C. Framework   D. Digital

4. Random access memory is considered _____ computer memory.   4. _B_
   A. non-volatile   B. volatile   C. cache   D. permanent

5. Which one of the following is NOT an operating system?   5. _D_
   A. Windows   B. IOS   C. Android   D. MS Office

6. A(n) _____ is a person who gets illegal access to a computer system and steals   6. _C_
   information.
   A. administrator   B. computer operator
   C. hacker   D. programmer

7. Which one of the following is NOT application software?   7. _C_
   A. MS Word   B. Media player
   C. Linux   D. MS Power Point

8. Which one of the following represents a domain name?   8. _A_
   A. .com   B. www   C. URL   D. HTTP

9. _____ is NOT an example of an Internet browser.   9. _B_
   A. Opera   B. Google
   C. Mozilla   D. Internet Explorer

10. Which one of the following is NOT a search engine?   10. _D_
    A. Altavista   B. Bing
    C. Yahoo   D. Facebook

11. E-mail is an abbreviation of   11. _A_
    A. electronic mail   B. easy mail
    C. electric email   D. both A and B

12. A(n) _____ is a person who takes care of websites for large companies.   12. B
    A. administrator   B. webmaster
    C. programmer   D. hacker

13. _____ connect web pages with each other.   13. C
    A. Connecters   B. Links   C. Hyperlinks   D. Browsers

14. _____ is a program that is harmful for computers.   14. B
    A. Spam   B. Virus
    C. Operating system   D. Plug-in

15. CC is an abbreviation of _____ in emails.   15. C
    A. core copy   B. copycat
    C. carbon copy   D. copy copy

16. Software most commonly used for basic personal computing is   16. A
    A. Excel   B. SPSS   C. Illustrator   D. Dreamweaver

17. _____ is an option to send the same letter to different persons.   17. C
    A. Template   B. Macros   C. Mail Merge   D. Layout

18. Which one of the following is a file extension for MS Word?   18. A
    A. .doc   B. .txt   C. .bmp   D. .pdf

19. _____ displays the number of words in a document.   19. B
    A. Character Count B. Word Count C. Word Wrap   D. Thesaurus

20. In an Excel sheet, an active cell is specified with   20. C
    A. dotted border   B. dark wide border
    C. italic text   D. a dotted border

21. A(n) _____ is a file that contains rows and columns.   21. B
    A. database   B. spreadsheet
    C. word   D. drawing

22. _____ are objects on the slides that hold text in a PowerPoint presentation.   22. A
    A. Placeholders   B. Text holders
    C. Auto layouts   D. Object holders

23. Which one of the following brings up the first slide in a PowerPoint presentation?   23. B
    A. Ctrl+End   B. Ctrl+Home
    C. Page up   D. Next slide button

24. Which one of the following sends printing commands to a printer?   24. B
    A. F5   B. Ctrl+P   C. Ctrl+S   D. F12

25. Scanners are used to capture _____ copy of documents.   25. B
    A. soft   B. hard   C. single   D. first

KEY (CORRECT ANSWERS)

1.	B		11.	A
2.	B		12.	B
3.	A		13.	C
4.	B		14.	B
5.	D		15.	C
6.	C		16.	A
7.	C		17.	C
8.	A		18.	A
9.	B		19.	B
10.	D		20.	B

21.	B
22.	A
23.	B
24.	B
25.	B

TEST 3

DIRECTIONS: Each question or incomplete statement is followed by several suggested answers or completions. Select the one that BEST answers the question or completes the statement. *PRINT THE LETTER OF THE CORRECT ANSWER IN THE SPACE AT THE RIGHT.*

1. Which one of the following is the MOST appropriate operation to move a text block in MS Word?
   A. Cut
   B. Save As
   C. Cut and Paste
   D. Copy and Paste

   1. C

2. The Navigation pane opens under the _____ tab.
   A. View
   B. Review
   C. Page Layout
   D. Mailings

   2. A

3. Ctrl+B makes selected test
   A. italic
   B. bold
   C. bigger
   D. uppercase

   3. C

4. _____ is NOT an acceptable formula in Excel.
   A. 10+50
   B. =10+50
   C. =B7+B8
   D. =B7*B8

   4. A

5. A worksheet usually contains _____ columns.
   A. 128
   B. 256
   C. 512
   D. 320

   5. B

6. _____ is the process of getting data from the cell that is located in different worksheets.
   A. Accessing
   B. Referencing
   C. Updating
   D. Functioning

   6. A

7. The shortcut _____ selects all PowerPoint slides at once.
   A. Ctrl+Home
   B. Ctrl+A
   C. Alt+Home
   D. Shift+A

   7. B

8. By pressing Ctrl+V in a Word document, the user
   A. pastes text
   B. cuts and pastes text
   C. adds a video box
   D. deletes a page

   8. A

9. Transitions are applicable only on
   A. Excel worksheets
   B. PowerPoint slides
   C. image files
   D. Word document

   9. ____

10. In MS Word, the _____ tab has options for margin, orientation and spacing.
    A. Design
    B. Review
    C. Page Layout
    D. Insert

    10. ____

11. Which one of the following is graphic software?
    A. MS Office
    B. Adobe Photoshop
    C. Firefox
    D. Notepad

    11. ____

12. Which one of the following is a social networking website?
    A. Facebook
    B. Yahoo
    C. Google
    D. ASK

    12. A

13. A computer monitor is referred to as a(n) _____ device.   13. A
    A. output   B. input   C. sound   D. printing

14. _____ memory is another name for the main memory of the computer.   14. A
    A. Primary   B. Direct   C. Simple   D. Quick

15. An operating system is _____ software.   15. B
    A. application   B. system   C. editing   D. both A and C

16. Which one of the following pieces of equipment is necessary for video calls?   16. A
    A. Webcam   B. Mouse   C. Scanner   D. Printer

17. _____ is a primary input device that is used to enter text and numbers.   17. B
    A. Mouse   B. Keyboard   C. Joystick   D. Microphone

18. Of the following, which is NOT an example of a web browser?   18. D
    A. Firefox   B. Opera   C. Chrome   D. Google Talk

19. A _____ is a collection of many web pages that are related to each other.   19. B
    A. web browser   B. website
    C. search engine   D. Firefox

20. Which one of the following is considered a personal journal used for posts?   20. A
    A. Blog   B. E-mail   C. Chat   D. Messengers

21. Windows _____ provides security against external threats.   21. D
    A. antivirus   B. spyware   C. firmware   D. firewall

22. Desktop and laptop computers are different from each other in terms of _____ and cost.   22. C
    A. operating system   B. functions
    C. physical structure   D. application software

23. _____ is a process of stealing confidential information without permission of the user.   23. B
    A. Forwarding   B. Hacking   C. Searching   D. Complaining

24. RAM is located in the _____ board.   24. C
    A. extension   B. external   C. mother   D. chip

25. All files on the computer are stored in   25. A
    A. hard drive   B. RAM
    C. cache   D. associative memory

KEY (CORRECT ANSWERS)

1.	C		11.	B
2.	A		12.	A
3.	B		13.	A
4.	A		14.	A
5.	B		15.	B
6.	B		16.	A
7.	B		17.	B
8.	A		18.	D
9.	B		19.	B
10.	C		20.	A

21.	D
22.	C
23.	B
24.	C
25.	A

TEST 4

DIRECTIONS: Each question or incomplete statement is followed by several suggested answers or completions. Select the one that BEST answers the question or completes the statement. *PRINT THE LETTER OF THE CORRECT ANSWER IN THE SPACE AT THE RIGHT.*

1. Which one of the following functions are performed by RAM?
   A. Read and Write
   B. Read
   C. Write
   D. Update

   1. A

2. _____ is an example of secondary storage.
   A. Diode   B. Hard disk   C. RAM   D. ROM

   2. B

3. USB is a type of _____ storage.
   A. primary   B. secondary   C. tertiary   D. temporary

   3. C

4. MPG file extension is used for _____ files.
   A. video   B. audio   C. image   D. flash

   4. A

5. .exe is an extension for _____ files.
   A. saved   B. executable   C. system   D. software

   5. B

6. Which one of the following is NOT a type of printer?
   A. Inkjet   B. Dot matrix   C. Laser   D. CRT

   6. D

7. _____ sends digital data across a phone line.
   A. Flash   B. Modem   C. NIC card   D. Keyboard

   7. B

8. _____ is a wireless technology used to transfer data among devices over short distances.
   A. USB   B. Modem   C. Wi-Fi   D. Bluetooth

   8. D

9. A user is listening to a song on his computer's music player. He is most likely listening to a(n) _____ file.
   A. .exe   B. .mus   C. .wav   D. .mp3

   9. D

10. PNG is an extension used for _____ files.
    A. audio   B. video   C. text   D. image

    10. D

11. Cache memory is located in the
    A. monitor   B. CPU   C. DVD   D. hard drive

    11. B

12. Computer resolution determines the number of
    A. colors   B. pixels   C. images   D. icons

    12. B

13. _____ is an extension used for images.
    A. GIF   B. MP3   C. MPG   D. PPT

    13. A

14. Which one of the following is NOT an e-mail server?
    A. Gmail   B. Yahoo   C. Chrome   D. Hotmail

14. C

15. _____ is an operating system developed by Apple.
    A. Mac IOS   B. Linux   C. Android   D. Windows

15. A

16. "What You See Is What You Get" (WYSIWYG) refers to
    A. editing text and graphics for web design
    B. buying a computer at a set price that can't be negotiated
    C. purchasing products as is on websites like Amazon and eBay
    D. printing web pages exactly as they appear on the screen

16. A

17. Which one of the following is the BEST option to add a new slide in an existing PowerPoint presentation?
    A. File, add a new slide   B. File, open
    C. Insert, new slide   D. File, new

17. C

18. _____ is the default setup for page orientation in PowerPoint.
    A. Horizontal   B. Vertical   C. Landscape   D. Portrait

18. C

19. Items in a list are typically shown by using
    A. graphics   B. bullets   C. icons   D. markers

19. B

20. In PowerPoint, _____ displays only text.
    A. outline view   B. slide show
    C. print view   D. slider sorter view

20. A

21. In Excel, a cell can be edited by use of
    A. a single click   B. a double click
    C. the format menu   D. formulas

21. A

22. Formulas are important features of Microsoft
    A. Word   B. PowerPoint   C. Excel   D. Publisher

22. C

23. In MS Word, which one of the following is used to underline a text?
    A. Ctrl+I   B. Ctrl+B   C. Ctrl+U   D. Ctrl+P

23. ____

24. Page color option can be found under the _____ tab.
    A. Page Layout   B. Design   C. Insert   D. View

24. ____

25. The F1 key typically displays a program's ____ menu.
    A. print   B. help
    C. tools   D. task manager

25. B

11

KEY (CORRECT ANSWERS)

1.	A		11.	B
2.	B		12.	B
3.	C		13.	A
4.	A		14.	C
5.	B		15.	A
6.	D		16.	A
7.	B		17.	C
8.	D		18.	C
9.	D		19.	B
10.	D		20.	A

21.	A
22.	C
23.	C
24.	B
25.	B

EXAMINATION SECTION

TEST 1

DIRECTIONS: Each question or incomplete statement is followed by several suggested answers or completions. Select the one that BEST answers the question or completes the statement. *PRINT THE LETTER OF THE CORRECT ANSWER IN THE SPACE AT THE RIGHT.*

1. The SDLC is defined as a process consisting of _____ phases.
   A. two   B. four   C. three   D. five

   1._D___

2. A framework that describes the set of activities performed at each stage of a software development project is
   A. SDLC   B. deployment
   C. waterfall model   D. SDLC model

   2._D___

3. How is noise defined in terms of software development?
   A. Writing irrelevant statement to the software development in the SRS document
   B. Adding clashing requirements in the SRS document
   C. Writing over-specific requirements
   D. Writing information about employees

   3._A___

4. Basically, a SWOT analysis is said to be a strategic
   A. analysis   B. measure   C. goal   D. alignment

   4._A___

5. In the system design phase of the SDLC, _____ is not part of the system's design phase.
   A. design of alternative systems
   B. writing a systems design report
   C. suggestions of alternative solutions
   D. selection of best system

   5._C___

6. In the system development life cycle, which of the following studies is conducted to determine the possible organizational resistance for a new system? _____ feasibility.
   A. Organizational   B. Operational   C. Economic   D. Employee

   6._B___

7. The _____ model is BEST suited when organization is very keen and motivated to identify the risk on early stages.
   A. waterfall   B. RAD   C. spiral   D. incremental

   7._C___

8. Scope of problem is defined with a
   A. critical path method (CPM) chart
   B. project evaluation and review technique (PERT) chart
   C. data flow diagram (DFD)
   D. context diagram

   8._D___

9. _____ is referred to as a method of database distribution in which different portions of the database reside at different nodes in the network.

    A. Splitting   B. Partitioning   C. Replication   D. Dividing

9. C

10. As a software associate, your client needs an information system that must communicate with existing systems. For that purpose, you need to adopt a design method and accurate linking with the existing system. Your designed system will be

    A. database   B. system interface
    C. help desks   D, design interface

10. B

11. In entity relation, when primary keys are linked with a foreign key, it forms a _____ relationship between the tables that connect them.

    A. many-to-many   B. one-to-one
    C. parent-child   D. server-and-client

11. C

12. In normalization, a relation is in a third normal form when no _____ attribute is determining another non-key attribute.

    A. dependent   B. non-key
    C. key   *Do I hafto learn this?*   D. none of the above

12. B

13. In library management databases, which terminology is used to refer to a specific record in your database?

    A. Relation   B. Instance   C. Table   D. Column

13. B

14. In database, a rule which describes that foreign key value must match with the primary key value in the other relationship is called

    A. referential integrity constraint   B. key match rule
    C. entity key group rule   D. foreign/primary match rule

14. A

15. The attribute on the left-hand side of the arrow in a functional dependency is known as

    A. candidate key   B. determinant
    C. foreign key   D. primary key

15. B

16. A report may be based on a

    A. table   B. query
    C. relations   D. both A and B

16. D

17. A software program which is used to build reports that summarize data from a database is known as

    A. report writer   B. reporter
    C. report builder   D. report generator

17. B

18. Which one of the following database objects is created FIRST?

    A. Table   B. Form   C. Report   D. Query

18. A

19. In data structures, a _____-linked list does not contain a null pointer at the end of the list.

    A. circular   B. doubly   C. null   D. stacked

    19. A

20. Polymorphism is described as the
    A. process of returning data from functions by reference
    B. specialization of classes through inheritance
    C. use of classes to represent objects
    D. packaging of data defining an object as a private member variable of class

    20. B

21. In C++, dynamic binding is useful for the functions that are
    A. overridden   B. defined once
    C. undefined   D. bounded

    21. A

22. In programming language, a function template is required when
    A. implementation details of function are independent of parameter data types
    B. all functions should be function templates
    C. two different functions have different implementation details
    D. two functions have the same type of parameters

    22. D

23. _____ are used to group classes for ease of use, maintainability and reusability.

    A. Use cases   B. States   C. Objects   D. Packages

    23. C

24. The description of structure and organization of data in database is contained in
    A. data dictionary   B. data mine
    C. structured query language   D. data mapping

    24. A

25. What is the output of the following programming code?

    ```
    Int p, q, r;
    P=10, q=3, r=2,
    If (p+q)<14&&(r<q-3)
    Cout <<r;
    Else
    Cout << p;
    ```

    A. -2   B. 4   C. 10   D. -4

    25. C

KEY (CORRECT ANSWERS)

1.	D		11.	C
2.	D		12.	B
3.	A		13.	B
4.	A		14.	A
5.	C		15.	B
6.	B		16.	D
7.	C		17.	B
8.	D		18.	A
9.	C		19.	A
10.	B		20.	B

21.	A
22.	D
23.	C
24.	A
25.	C

_____

TEST 2

DIRECTIONS: Each question or incomplete statement is followed by several suggested answers or completions. Select the one that BEST answers the question or completes the statement. *PRINT THE LETTER OF THE CORRECT ANSWER IN THE SPACE AT THE RIGHT.*

1. Which of the following is the BEST fact-finding technique that is most helpful in collecting quantitative data?
   A. Interviews
   B. Record reviews and comparisons
   C. Questionnaires
   D. Workshops

   1. C

2. _____ data is a type of data collected from open-ended questions.
   A. Quantitative
   B. Qualitative
   C. Experimental
   D. Non-official

   2. B

3. Usually a feasibility study is carried out
   A. after completion of final requirement specification
   B. before the start of the project
   C. before the completion of final requirements specifications
   D. at any time

   3. A

4. In the analysis phase, which diagram is used to present declaration of the goals and objectives of the project.
   A. Data flow diagram
   B. Entity relationship diagram
   C. Flowchart
   D. Documentation

   4. C

5. In SDLC, _____ is used to ensure that no alternative is ignored during data analysis.
   A. data flow diagram
   B. organizational chart
   C. Gantt chart
   D. decision table

   5. D

6. Which of the following software is used to measure hardware and software alternatives?
   A. Automated design tools
   B. DFD
   C. Report generators
   D. Project management

   6. A

7. _____ is responsible to write Software Requirement Specifications Document (SRS).
   A. Project manager
   B. System analyst
   C. Programmer
   D. User

   7. A

8. An entity which relates to itself in an ERD model is referred to as _____ relationship.
   A. recursive
   B. one-to-many
   C. many-to-many
   D. one-to-one

   8. A

9. The goal of normalization is
   A. to increase the number of relations
   B. to increase redundancy
   C. independence of any other relation
   D. to get stable data structure

9. D

10. CMM stands for
    A. Capability Maturity Model
    B. Configuration Maturity Model
    C. Capacity Building Manager
    D. Company Management Method

10. A

11. Data _____ is terminology used for data accuracy and completeness in any database.
    A. constraint   B. redundancy   C. model   D. integrity

11. D

12. A candidate key is defined as
    A. a primary key
    B. the primary key selected to be the key of a relation
    C. an attribute or group of attributes that can be a primary key
    D. both A and B

12. C

13. The ability of a class to derive the properties from previously defined class is
    A. encapsulation
    B. polymorphism
    C. information hiding
    D. inheritance

13. D

14. A queue data structure stores and retrieves items in a _____ manner.
    A. last in, first out
    B. first in, last out
    C. first in, first out
    D. last in, last out

14. C

15. The process of writing a program from an algorithm is called
    A. coding   B. decoding   C. encoding   D. encrypting

15. A

16. The CORRECT sequence for creating and executing C++ program is:
    A. Compiling-Editing-Saving-Executing-Linking
    B. Editing-Executing-Compiling-Linking
    C. Editing-Saving-Compiling-Linking-Executing
    D. Linking-Executing-Saving-Compiling

16. C

17. As an instructor, you have given your class a programming problem.
    Every student comes up with a different instruction code for the same problem.
    Suppose one student has a code of 50 lines, while another has a code of 100 instructions for the same problem.
    Which of the following statements is TRUE?
    A. The greater execution time is required for more instructions than that of less instructions.
    B. Execution time of all programs are the same.
    C. The number of instruction codes does not affect the solution.
    D. Compilation time is greater with more numbers of instruction.

17. A

18. In programming languages, a counter can be defined as
    A. the final value of a loop
    B. a variable that counts loop iterations
    C. the initial value of a loop
    D. the stop value of loop

18. B

19. Which reserve word is used in programming languages to move the control back to the start of the loop body?
    A. Break   B. Go to   C. Continue   D. Switch

19. C

20. The FIRST line in switch block contains the
    A. value of first criterion
    B. statement to be executed if the first criteria is true
    C. expression to be evaluated
    D. statement to be executed if none of the criteria is true

20. B

21. What is the output of the following code?

```
int main ()
{
    int a = 19;
    {
        cout << "value of a: "<<a<<endl;
        a = a + 1;
    }while(a<20);
    return 0;
}
```

    A. 19   B. 20   C. 11   D. 100

21. A

22. A computer dedicated to screening access to a network from outside the network is known as
    A. hot site   B. cold site   C. firewall   D. vaccine

22. C

23. In anticipation of physical destruction, every organization should have a
    A. biometric scheme   B. disaster recovery plan
    C. DES   D. set of active plan

23. B

24. Debug is a term denoting
    A. error correction process
    B. writing of instructions in developing a new program
    C. fault detection in equipment
    D. determine useful life

24. A

25. A feature of word processing software to link the name and addresses with a standard document is called
    A. mail merge   B. database management
    C. references   D. review/comment

25. A

KEY (CORRECT ANSWERS)

1.	C		11.	D
2.	B		12.	C
3.	A		13.	D
4.	C		14.	C
5.	D		15.	A
6.	A		16.	C
7.	A		17.	A
8.	A		18.	B
9.	D		19.	C
10.	A		20.	B

21.	A
22.	C
23.	B
24.	A
25.	A

TEST 3

DIRECTIONS: Each question or incomplete statement is followed by several suggested answers or completions. Select the one that BEST answers the question or completes the statement. *PRINT THE LETTER OF THE CORRECT ANSWER IN THE SPACE AT THE RIGHT.*

1. The parallelogram symbol in a flow chart indicates a
   A. process   B. progress   C. condition   D. input/output

   1. _D_

2. A feasibility study in SDLC performs
   A. cost/benefit analysis
   B. designing technique analysis
   C. debugging selection
   D. programming language selection

   2. _A_

3. Who is responsible for performing the feasibility study?
   A. Organizational managers
   B. Both organizational manager and system analyst
   C. Users of the proposed system
   D. Both perspective user and systems designers

   3. _A_

4. A study of employees' working habits, phobias and obsessions during implementation of a new system is called _____ analysis.
   A. personality   B. cultural feasibility
   C. economic feasibility   D. technological feasibility

   4. _B_

5. As a software associate, a(n) _____ model is based on a regression testing technique.
   A. waterfall   B. RAD   C. V   D. iterative

   5. _D_

6. The adaptable model which describes features of the proposed system and is implemented before the installation of the actual system is known as
   A. JAD   B. template   C. RAD   D. prototype

   6. _D_

7. Milestones in system development life cycle represent
   A. cost of project   B. status of project
   C. user expectation   D. final product of project

   7. _B_

8. Scheduling deadlines and milestones can be shown on a
   A. system survey   B. decision table
   C. prototype   D. Gantt chart

   8. _D_

9. Suppose your current organization wants to expand its business into different cities. For that purpose, it needs to distribute business applications across multiple locations. For example, computer systems, storing the data center for Web server, database and telecommunication functions. This is an example of

9. _B_

    A. applications architecture planning
    B. technology architecture planning
    C. enterprise resource planning (ERP)
    D. strategic planning

10. All of the following are components of a physical database EXCEPT

10. _D_

    A. file organization   B. data volume
    C. data distribution   D. normalize the relations

11. Suppose working as a computer associate your organization has assigned you a task to develop a database for an academic institution. Which one is the MOST appropriate association in the database for a class that might have multiple prerequisites?

11. _D_

    A. Generalization association   B. N-ary association
    C. Aggregation association   D. Reflexive association

12. While working on an academic institute database, according to you, which one is the MOST suitable special association to model a course that has an instructor, teaching assistants, a classroom, meeting time slot and class schedule?

12. _B_

    A. Generalization association   B. N-ary association
    C. Aggregation association   D. Reflexive association

13. Which one of the following is the MOST suitable association that shows that multiple textbooks for a course are required to make a reading list?

13. _C_

    A. Aggregation association   B. Generalization association
    C. N-ary association   D. Reflexive association

14. In parameters, passing by value

14. _A_

    A. actual parameters and formal parameters must be similar types
    B. actual parameters and formal parameters can be different types
    C. parameters passing by value can be used both for input and output purpose
    D. both A and B

15. In data structures, which of the following can be used to facilitate adding nodes to the end of the linear linked list?

15. _C_

    A. Head pointer   B. Zero head node
    C. Tail pointer   D. Precede pointer

16. A full binary tree with n leaves consist of _____ nodes.

16. _B_

    A. n   B. 2^{n-1} C. n-1   D. log n

17. Linear model and prototyping model are combined to form a _____ model.
    A. waterfall
    B. incremental
    C. build & fix
    D. spiral

    17. B

18. An example of query is
    A. selection of all records that match a set of criteria
    B. importing spreadsheet file into the database
    C. search for specific record
    D. both A and C are correct

    18. D

19. The database development process involves mapping of conceptual data model into a(n) _____ model.
    A. object-oriented
    B. network data
    C. implementation
    D. hierarchical data

    19. C

20. In database, one field or combination of fields for which more than one record may have the same combination of values is called the
    A. secondary key
    B. index
    C. composite key
    D. linked key

    20. A

21. Customers, cars and parts are examples of
    A. entities
    B. attributes
    C. cardinals
    D. relationships

    21. A

22. A ping program used to send a multiple packet to a server to check its ability to handle a quantity of traffic maliciously is called
    A. pagejacking
    B. jam sync
    C. ping storm
    D. ping strangeness

    22. C

23. Which one of the following is the key factor to develop a new system to manage a disaster?
    A. Equipment replacement
    B. Unfavorable weather
    C. Lack of insurance coverage
    D. Loss of processing ability

    23. D

24. As a computer associate, you ask 100 client organization employees to fill out a survey that includes questions about educational background, their job type, salary and amount spent on purchases of a widget annually. After you enter the data in a spreadsheet program, you decide to look for a relationship between income and the amount spent on widgets. The BEST way to display the data for this kind of assumption is a _____ chart.
    A. bullet
    B. line
    C. pic
    D. scatter

    24. D

25. Suppose it is your very first day of your job. When you turn on your computer, the system unit is visibly on but the monitor is dark. What is the exact issue?
    A. The monitor model is too old to work
    B. The operating system is not working
    C. The monitor is not connected to the PC
    D. Call the help desk officer

    25. C

KEY (CORRECT ANSWERS)

1.	D		11.	D
2.	A		12.	B
3.	A		13.	C
4.	B		14.	A
5.	D		15.	C
6.	D		16.	B
7.	B		17.	B
8.	D		18.	D
9.	B		19.	C
10.	D		20.	A

21.	A
22.	C
23.	D
24.	D
25.	C

TEST 4

DIRECTIONS: Each question or incomplete statement is followed by several suggested answers or completions. Select the one that BEST answers the question or completes the statement. *PRINT THE LETTER OF THE CORRECT ANSWER IN THE SPACE AT THE RIGHT.*

1. A collection of logically related data elements that can be used for multiple processing needs is called
   A. files   B. a register   C. a database   D. organization

       1._____

2. For the purpose of data gathering, your organization and client have secretly engaged you in the client group that is being studied. You are considered a(n)
   A. observer-as-participant   B. observer
   C. complete participant   D. part-time employee

       2._____

3. For data gathering, interviews in which the topics are pre-decided but the sequence and phrasing can be adapted during the interview is called a(n)
   A. informal conversational interview
   B. closed quantitative interview
   C. standardized open-ended interview
   D. interview-guided approach

       3._____

4. In SDLC, which of the following analysis methods is adopted to start with the "intricate image" and then breaks it down into smaller sections?
   A. Financial   B. Bottom up   C. Reverse
   D. Top-down   E. Executive

       4._____

5. As a software associate, which one of the following is the biggest reason for the failure of system development projects?
   A. Lack of JAD sessions
   B. Purchasing COTS
   C. Imprecise or missing business requirements
   D. Hurdles from employees

       5._____

6. The _____ model is the BEST suited model to create client/server applications.
   A. waterfall   B. spiral   C. incremental   D. concurrent

       6._____

7. Which hardware component is essential for function of a database management system?
   A. Larger capacity, high speed disk
   B. Mouse
   C. High resolution monitors
   D. Printer

       7._____

8. _____ refers to a method of database distribution in which one database contains data that are included in another database.
   A. Splitting   B. Partitioning
   C. Replication   D. Dividing

       8._____

9. In the database design process, which one of the following is referred to modality?
   A. Optional
   B. Mandatory
   C. Unidirectional
   D. Both A and B

9.____

10. According to the research conducted by an international professional organization, out of 100 most occupied jobs that they researched, the top job classification was a
    A. database administrator
    B. cryptographer
    C. programmer
    D. computer engineer

10.____

11. In the database, different attributes in two different tables having the same name are referred to as
    A. a synonym
    B. a homonym
    C. an acronym
    D. mutually exclusive

11.____

12. Consider two tables: Class and Student are related by a "one-to-many" relationship. In which table should the corresponding foreign key be placed?
    A. Only Class table requires foreign key.
    B. Only Student table requires foreign key.
    C. Both tables require foreign key.
    D. Composite entity must be added so foreign keys will be required in both Class and Student tables.

12.____

13.

13.____

Using the above E-R diagram, which one of the following statements is TRUE?
    A. Both tables should have the same number of (primary) key attributes.
    B. Table A should have a larger number of key attributes.
    C. Table B should have a larger number of key attributes.
    D. The diagram does not propose which table might have more attributes in its primary key.

14. Which form of functional dependency is the set of attributes that is neither a subset or any of the keys nor the candidate key?
    A. Full functional dependency
    B. Partial dependency
    C. Primary functional dependency
    D. Transitive dependency

14.____

15. The true dependencies are formed by the _____ rule.
    A. reflexive
    B. referential
    C. inferential
    D. termination

15.____

16. Which facility helps DBMS to synchronize its files and journals while occasionally suspending all processing?
    A. Checkpoint facility
    B. Backup recovery
    C. Recovery manager
    D. Database change log

16.____

17. In data structures, which one of the following operations is used to retrieve
    and then remove the top of the stack?
    A. Create Stack   B. Push
    C. Pop   D. Pull

17.____

18. Class definition
    A. must have a constructor specified
    B. must end with a semicolon
    C. provides the class interface
    D. both B and C

18.____

19. Which operator is used in compound condition to join two conditions?
    A. Relational operator   B. Logical operator
    C. Relational result   D. Logical result

19.____

20. The conditional portion of IF statements can contain any
    A. valid expression
    B. expression that can be evaluated to Boolean value
    C. valid variable
    D. valid constant or variable

20.____

21. System analysts suggest that telecommuting will become more popular with
    managers and client teams when
    A. workers are forced to telecommute
    B. the manager finally gives up the idea of controlling the worker
    C. multimedia teleconferencing system becomes affordable
    D. automobiles become outdated

21.____

22. Error reports are an example of _____ reports.
    A. scheduled   B. exception   C. on-demand   D. external

22.____

23. Word processing, electronic filling, and electronic mails are part of
    A. help desk   B. electronic industry
    C. office automation   D. official tasks

23.____

24. In a word processor, the block that appears at the top and bottom of
    every page which display deals is called the
    A. top and bottom margin   B. headline and end note
    C. title and page number   D. header and footer

24.____

25. In word processing software, _____ are inserted as a cross-reference.
    A. placeholders   B. bookmarks   C. objects   D. word fields

25.____

KEY (CORRECT ANSWERS)

1.	C		11.	C
2.	C		12.	B
3.	D		13.	D
4.	B		14.	D
5.	C		15.	A
6.	D		16.	A
7.	A		17.	C
8.	C		18.	A
9.	D		19.	D
10.	D		20.	A

21.	C
22.	B
23.	C
24.	D
25.	D

EXAMINATION SECTION

TEST 1

DIRECTIONS: Each question or incomplete statement is followed by several suggested answers or completions. Select the one that BEST answers the question or completes the statement. *PRINT THE LETTER OF THE CORRECT ANSWER IN THE SPACE AT THE RIGHT.*

1. Which of the following is the BEST fact-finding technique that is most helpful in collecting quantitative data?
   A. Interviews
   B. Record reviews and comparisons
   C. Questionnaires
   D. Workshops

1.____

2. _____ data is a type of data collected from open-ended questions.
   A. Quantitative
   B. Qualitative
   C. Experimental
   D. Non-official

2.____

3. Usually a feasibility study is carried out
   A. after completion of final requirement specification
   B. before the start of the project
   C. before the completion of final requirements specifications
   D. at any time

3.____

4. In the analysis phase, which diagram is used to present declaration of the goals and objectives of the project.
   A. Data flow diagram
   B. Entity relationship diagram
   C. Flowchart
   D. Documentation

4.____

5. In SDLC, _____ is used to ensure that no alternative is ignored during data analysis.
   A. data flow diagram
   B. organizational chart
   C. Gantt chart
   D. decision table

5.____

6. Which of the following software is used to measure hardware and software alternatives?
   A. Automated design tools
   B. DFD
   C. Report generators
   D. Project management

6.____

7. _____ is responsible to write Software Requirement Specifications Document (SRS).
   A. Project manager
   B. System analyst
   C. Programmer
   D. User

7.____

8. An entity which relates to itself in an ERD model is referred to as _____ relationship.
   A. recursive
   B. one-to-many
   C. many-to-many
   D. one-to-one

8.____

9. The goal of normalization is   9.____
   A. to increase the number of relations
   B. to increase redundancy
   C. independence of any other relation
   D. to get stable data structure

10. CMM stands for   10.____
    A. Capability Maturity Model   B. Configuration Maturity Model
    C. Capacity Building Manager   D. Company Management Method

11. Data _____ is terminology used for data accuracy and completeness in any   11.____
    database.
    A. constraint   B. redundancy   C. model   D. integrity

12. A candidate key is defined as   12.____
    A. a primary key
    B. the primary key selected to be the key of a relation
    C. an attribute or group of attributes that can be a primary key
    D. both A and B

13. The ability of a class to derive the properties from previously defined class   13.____
    is
    A. encapsulation   B. polymorphism
    C. information hiding   D. inheritance

14. A queue data structure stores and retrieves items in a _____ manner.   14.____
    A. last in, first out   B. first in, last out
    C. first in, first out   D. last in, last out

15. The process of writing a program from an algorithm is called   15.____
    A. coding   B. decoding   C. encoding   D. encrypting

16. The CORRECT sequence for creating and executing C++ program is: 16.____
    A. Compiling-Editing-Saving-Executing-Linking
    B. Editing-Executing-Compiling-Linking
    C. Editing-Saving-Compiling-Linking-Executing
    D. Linking-Executing-Saving-Compiling

17. As an instructor, you have given your class a programming problem.   17.____
    Every student comes up with a different instruction code for the same problem.
    Suppose one student has a code of 50 lines, while another has a code of 100
    instructions for the same problem.
    Which of the following statements is TRUE?
    A. The greater execution time is required for more instructions than that of
       less instructions.
    B. Execution time of all programs are the same.
    C. The number of instruction codes does not affect the solution.
    D. Compilation time is greater with more numbers of instruction.

18. In programming languages, a counter can be defined as
    A. the final value of a loop
    B. a variable that counts loop iterations
    C. the initial value of a loop
    D. the stop value of loop

18.____

19. Which reserve word is used in programming languages to move the control back to the start of the loop body?
    A. Break   B. Go to   C. Continue   D. Switch

19.____

20. The FIRST line in switch block contains the
    A. value of first criterion
    B. statement to be executed if the first criteria is true
    C. expression to be evaluated
    D. statement to be executed if none of the criteria is true

20.____

21. What is the output of the following code?

```
int main ()
{
    int a = 19;
    {
        cout << "value of a: "<<a<<endl;
        a = a + 1;
    }while(a<20);
    return 0;
}
```

    A. 19   B. 20   C. 11   D. 100

21.____

22. A computer dedicated to screening access to a network from outside the network is known as
    A. hot site   B. cold site   C. firewall   D. vaccine

22.____

23. In anticipation of physical destruction, every organization should have a
    A. biometric scheme   B. disaster recovery plan
    C. DES   D. set of active plan

23.____

24. Debug is a term denoting
    A. error correction process
    B. writing of instructions in developing a new program
    C. fault detection in equipment
    D. determine useful life

24.____

25. A feature of word processing software to link the name and addresses with a standard document is called
    A. mail merge   B. database management
    C. references   D. review/comment

25.____

KEY (CORRECT ANSWERS)

1.	C		11.	D
2.	B		12.	C
3.	A		13.	D
4.	C		14.	C
5.	D		15.	A
6.	A		16.	C
7.	A		17.	A
8.	A		18.	B
9.	D		19.	C
10.	A		20.	B

21.	A
22.	C
23.	B
24.	A
25.	A

_____

TEST 2

DIRECTIONS: Each question or incomplete statement is followed by several suggested answers or completions. Select the one that BEST answers the question or completes the statement. *PRINT THE LETTER OF THE CORRECT ANSWER IN THE SPACE AT THE RIGHT.*

1. The SDLC is defined as a process consisting of _____ phases.
   A. two   B. four   C. three   D. five

1.____

2. A framework that describes the set of activities performed at each stage of a software development project is
   A. SDLC   B. deployment
   C. waterfall model   D. SDLC model

2.____

3. How is noise defined in terms of software development?
   A. Writing irrelevant statement to the software development in the SRS document
   B. Adding clashing requirements in the SRS document
   C. Writing over-specific requirements
   D. Writing information about employees

3.____

4. Basically, a SWOT analysis is said to be a strategic
   A. analysis   B. measure   C. goal   D. alignment

4.____

5. In the system design phase of the SDLC, _____ is not part of the system's design phase.
   A. design of alternative systems
   B. writing a systems design report
   C. suggestions of alternative solutions
   D. selection of best system

5.____

6. In the system development life cycle, which of the following studies is conducted to determine the possible organizational resistance for a new system? _____ feasibility.
   A. Organizational   B. Operational   C. Economic   D. Employee

6.____

7. The _____ model is BEST suited when organization is very keen and motivated to identify the risk on early stages.
   A. waterfall   B. RAD   C. spiral   D. incremental

7.____

8. Scope of problem is defined with a
   A. critical path method (CPM) chart
   B. project evaluation and review technique (PERT) chart
   C. data flow diagram (DFD)
   D. context diagram

8.____

9. _____ is referred to as a method of database distribution in which different portions of the database reside at different nodes in the network. 9.____
   A. Splitting   B. Partitioning   C. Replication   D. Dividing

10. As a computer specialist (software), your client needs an information system that must communicate with existing systems. For that purpose, you need to adopt a design method and accurate linking with the existing system. Your designed system will be 10.____
   A. database   B. system interface
   C. help desks   D, design interface

11. In entity relation, when primary keys are linked with a foreign key, it forms a _____ relationship between the tables that connect them. 11.____
   A. many-to-many   B. one-to-one
   C. parent-child   D. server-and-client

12. In normalization, a relation is in a third normal form when no _____ attribute is determining another non-key attribute. 12.____
   A. dependent   B. non-key
   C. key   D. none of the above

13. In library management databases, which terminology is used to refer to a specific record in your database? 13.____
   A. Relation   B. Instance   C. Table   D. Column

14. In database, a rule which describes that foreign key value must match with the primary key value in the other relationship is called 14.____
   A. referential integrity constraint   B. key match rule
   C. entity key group rule   D. foreign/primary match rule

15. The attribute on the left-hand side of the arrow in a functional dependency is known as 15.____
   A. candidate key   B. determinant
   C. foreign key   D. primary key

16. A report may be based on a 16.____
   A. table   B. query
   C. relations   D. both A and B

17. A software program which is used to build reports that summarize data from a database is known as 17.____
   A. report writer   B. reporter
   C. report builder   D. report generator

18. Which one of the following database objects is created FIRST? 18.____
   A. Table   B. Form   C. Report   D. Query

19. In data structures, a _____-linked list does not contain a null pointer at the end of the list.

    A. circular   B. doubly   C. null   D. stacked

    19.____

20. Polymorphism is described as the
    A. process of returning data from functions by reference
    B. specialization of classes through inheritance
    C. use of classes to represent objects
    D. packaging of data defining an object as a private member variable of class

    20.____

21. In C++, dynamic binding is useful for the functions that are
    A. overridden   B. defined once
    C. undefined   D. bounded

    21.____

22. In programming language, a function template is required when
    A. implementation details of function are independent of parameter data types
    B. all functions should be function templates
    C. two different functions have different implementation details
    D. two functions have the same type of parameters

    22.____

23. _____ are used to group classes for ease of use, maintainability and reusability.
    A. Use cases   B. States   C. Objects   D. Packages

    23.____

24. The description of structure and organization of data in database is contained in
    A. data dictionary   B. data mine
    C. structured query language   D. data mapping

    24.____

25. What is the output of the following programming code?

```
Int p, q, r;
P=10, q=3, r=2,
If (p+q)<14&&(r<q-3)
Cout <<r;
Else
Cout << p;
```

    A. -2   B. 4   C. 10   D. -4

    25.____

_____

KEY (CORRECT ANSWERS)

1.	D		11.	C
2.	D		12.	B
3.	A		13.	B
4.	A		14.	A
5.	C		15.	B
6.	B		16.	D
7.	C		17.	B
8.	D		18.	A
9.	C		19.	A
10.	B		20.	B

21. A
22. D
23. C
24. A
25. C

———

TEST 3

DIRECTIONS: Each question or incomplete statement is followed by several suggested answers or completions. Select the one that BEST answers the question or completes the statement. *PRINT THE LETTER OF THE CORRECT ANSWER IN THE SPACE AT THE RIGHT.*

1. The parallelogram symbol in a flow chart indicates a
   A. process   B. progress   C. condition   D. input/output

   1._____

2. A feasibility study in SDLC performs
   A. cost/benefit analysis
   B. designing technique analysis
   C. debugging selection
   D. programming language selection

   2._____

3. Who is responsible for performing the feasibility study?
   A. Organizational managers
   B. Both organizational manager and system analyst
   C. Users of the proposed system
   D. Both perspective user and systems designers

   3._____

4. A study of employees' working habits, phobias and obsessions during implementation of a new system is called _____ analysis.
   A. personality   B. cultural feasibility
   C. economic feasibility   D. technological feasibility

   4._____

5. As a computer specialist (software), a(n) _____ model is based on a regression testing technique.
   A. waterfall   B. RAD   C. V   D. iterative

   5._____

6. The adaptable model which describes features of the proposed system and is implemented before the installation of the actual system is known as
   A. JAD   B. template   C. RAD   D. prototype

   6._____

7. Milestones in system development life cycle represent
   A. cost of project   B. status of project
   C. user expectation   D. final product of project

   7._____

8. Scheduling deadlines and milestones can be shown on a
   A. system survey   B. decision table
   C. prototype   D. Gantt chart

   8._____

9. Suppose your current organization wants to expand its business into different cities. For that purpose, it needs to distribute business applications across multiple locations. For example, computer systems, storing the data center for Web server, database and telecommunication functions. This is an example of

    A. applications architecture planning
    B. technology architecture planning
    C. enterprise resource planning (ERP)
    D. strategic planning

9.____

10. All of the following are components of a physical database EXCEPT

    A. file organization   B. data volume
    C. data distribution   D. normalize the relations

10.____

11. Suppose working as a computer specialist (software) your organization has assigned you a task to develop a database for an academic institution. Which one is the MOST appropriate association in the database for a class that might have multiple prerequisites?

    A. Generalization association   B. N-ary association
    C. Aggregation association   D. Reflexive association

11.____

12. While working on an academic institute database, according to you, which one is the MOST suitable special association to model a course that has an instructor, teaching assistants, a classroom, meeting time slot and class schedule?

    A. Generalization association   B. N-ary association
    C. Aggregation association   D. Reflexive association

12.____

13. Which one of the following is the MOST suitable association that shows that multiple textbooks for a course are required to make a reading list?

    A. Aggregation association   B. Generalization association
    C. N-ary association   D. Reflexive association

13.____

14. In parameters, passing by value

    A. actual parameters and formal parameters must be similar types
    B. actual parameters and formal parameters can be different types
    C. parameters passing by value can be used both for input and output purpose
    D. both A and B

14.____

15. In data structures, which of the following can be used to facilitate adding nodes to the end of the linear linked list?

    A. Head pointer   B. Zero head node
    C. Tail pointer   D. Precede pointer

15.____

16. A full binary tree with n leaves consist of _____ nodes.

    A. n   B. 2^{n-1} C. n-1   D. log n

16.____

17. Linear model and prototyping model are combined to form a _____ model.
   A. waterfall
   B. incremental
   C. build & fix
   D. spiral

17.____

18. An example of query is
   A. selection of all records that match a set of criteria
   B. importing spreadsheet file into the database
   C. search for specific record
   D. both A and C are correct

18.____

19. The database development process involves mapping of conceptual data model into a(n) _____ model.
   A. object-oriented
   B. network data
   C. implementation
   D. hierarchical data

19.____

20. In database, one field or combination of fields for which more than one record may have the same combination of values is called the
   A. secondary key
   B. index
   C. composite key
   D. linked key

20.____

21. Customers, cars and parts are examples of
   A. entities
   B. attributes
   C. cardinals
   D. relationships

21.____

22. A ping program used to send a multiple packet to a server to check its ability to handle a quantity of traffic maliciously is called
   A. pagejacking
   B. jam sync
   C. ping storm
   D. ping strangeness

22.____

23. Which one of the following is the key factor to develop a new system to manage a disaster?
   A. Equipment replacement
   B. Unfavorable weather
   C. Lack of insurance coverage
   D. Loss of processing ability

23.____

24. As a computer specialist (software), you ask 100 client organization employees to fill out a survey that includes questions about educational background, their job type, salary and amount spent on purchases of a widget annually. After you enter the data in a spreadsheet program, you decide to look for a relationship between income and the amount spent on widgets. The BEST way to display the data for this kind of assumption is a _____ chart.
   A. bullet
   B. line
   C. pic
   D. scatter

24.____

25. Suppose it is your very first day of your job. When you turn on your computer, the system unit is visibly on but the monitor is dark. What is the exact issue?
   A. The monitor model is too old to work
   B. The operating system is not working
   C. The monitor is not connected to the PC
   D. Call the help desk officer

25.____

KEY (CORRECT ANSWERS)

1.	D		11.	D
2.	A		12.	B
3.	A		13.	C
4.	B		14.	A
5.	D		15.	C
6.	D		16.	B
7.	B		17.	B
8.	D		18.	D
9.	B		19.	C
10.	D		20.	A

21.	A
22.	C
23.	D
24.	D
25.	C

TEST 4

DIRECTIONS: Each question or incomplete statement is followed by several suggested answers or completions. Select the one that BEST answers the question or completes the statement. *PRINT THE LETTER OF THE CORRECT ANSWER IN THE SPACE AT THE RIGHT.*

1. A collection of logically related data elements that can be used for multiple processing needs is called
   A. files   B. a register   C. a database   D. organization

   1.____

2. For the purpose of data gathering, your organization and client have secretly engaged you in the client group that is being studied. You are considered a(n)
   A. observer-as-participant   B. observer
   C. complete participant   D. part-time employee

   2.____

3. For data gathering, interviews in which the topics are pre-decided but the sequence and phrasing can be adapted during the interview is called a(n)
   A. informal conversational interview
   B. closed quantitative interview
   C. standardized open-ended interview
   D. interview-guided approach

   3.____

4. In SDLC, which of the following analysis methods is adopted to start with the "intricate image" and then breaks it down into smaller sections?
   A. Financial   B. Bottom up   C. Reverse
   D. Top-down   E. Executive

   4.____

5. As a computer specialist (software), which one of the following is the biggest reason for the failure of system development projects?
   A. Lack of JAD sessions
   B. Purchasing COTS
   C. Imprecise or missing business requirements
   D. Hurdles from employees

   5.____

6. The _____ model is the BEST suited model to create client/server applications.
   A. waterfall   B. spiral   C. incremental   D. concurrent

   6.____

7. Which hardware component is essential for function of a database management system?
   A. Larger capacity, high speed disk
   B. Mouse
   C. High resolution monitors
   D. Printer

   7.____

8. _____ refers to a method of database distribution in which one database contains data that are included in another database.
   A. Splitting   B. Partitioning
   C. Replication   D. Dividing

   8.____

9. In the database design process, which one of the following is referred to modality?

    A. Optional   B. Mandatory

    C. Unidirectional   D. Both A and B

9._____

10. According to the research conducted by an international professional organization, out of 100 most occupied jobs that they researched, the top job classification was a

    A. database administrator   B. cryptographer

    C. programmer   D. computer engineer

10._____

11. In the database, different attributes in two different tables having the same name are referred to as

    A. a synonym   B. a homonym

    C. an acronym   D. mutually exclusive

11._____

12. Consider two tables: Class and Student are related by a "one-to-many" relationship. In which table should the corresponding foreign key be placed?

    A. Only Class table requires foreign key.

    B. Only Student table requires foreign key.

    C. Both tables require foreign key.

    D. Composite entity must be added so foreign keys will be required in both Class and Student tables.

12._____

13.

Using the above E-R diagram, which one of the following statements is TRUE?

    A. Both tables should have the same number of (primary) key attributes.

    B. Table A should have a larger number of key attributes.

    C. Table B should have a larger number of key attributes.

    D. The diagram does not propose which table might have more attributes in its primary key.

13._____

14. Which form of functional dependency is the set of attributes that is neither a subset or any of the keys nor the candidate key?

    A. Full functional dependency   B. Partial dependency

    C. Primary functional dependency   D. Transitive dependency

14._____

15. The true dependencies are formed by the _____ rule.

    A. reflexive   B. referential   C. inferential   D. termination

15._____

16. Which facility helps DBMS to synchronize its files and journals while occasionally suspending all processing?

    A. Checkpoint facility   B. Backup recovery

    C. Recovery manager   D. Database change log

16._____

17. In data structures, which one of the following operations is used to retrieve and then remove the top of the stack?
    A. Create Stack   B. Push
    C. Pop   D. Pull

17.____

18. Class definition
    A. must have a constructor specified
    B. must end with a semicolon
    C. provides the class interface
    D. both B and C

18.____

19. Which operator is used in compound condition to join two conditions?
    A. Relational operator   B. Logical operator
    C. Relational result   D. Logical result

19.____

20. The conditional portion of IF statements can contain any
    A. valid expression
    B. expression that can be evaluated to Boolean value
    C. valid variable
    D. valid constant or variable

20.____

21. System analysts suggest that telecommuting will become more popular with managers and client teams when
    A. workers are forced to telecommute
    B. the manager finally gives up the idea of controlling the worker
    C. multimedia teleconferencing system becomes affordable
    D. automobiles become outdated

21.____

22. Error reports are an example of _____ reports.
    A. scheduled   B. exception   C. on-demand   D. external

22.____

23. Word processing, electronic filling, and electronic mails are part of
    A. help desk   B. electronic industry
    C. office automation   D. official tasks

23.____

24. In a word processor, the block that appears at the top and bottom of every page which display deals is called the
    A. top and bottom margin   B. headline and end note
    C. title and page number   D. header and footer

24.____

25. In word processing software, _____ are inserted as a cross-reference.
    A. placeholders   B. bookmarks   C. objects   D. word fields

25.____

KEY (CORRECT ANSWERS)

1.	C		11.	C
2.	C		12.	B
3.	D		13.	D
4.	B		14.	D
5.	C		15.	A
6.	D		16.	A
7.	A		17.	C
8.	C		18.	A
9.	D		19.	D
10.	D		20.	A

21.	C
22.	B
23.	C
24.	D
25.	D

EXAMINATION SECTION

TEST 1

DIRECTIONS: Each question or incomplete statement is followed by several suggested answers or completions. Select the one that BEST answers the question or completes the statement. *PRINT THE LETTER OF THE CORRECT ANSWER IN THE SPACE AT THE RIGHT.*

1. What is VGA?
   A. Video Graphics Array
   B. Video Graphics Adapter
   C. Visual Graphics Array
   D. None of the above

   1._____

2. IBM 1401 was a
   A. fourth generation computer
   B. second generation computer
   C. third generation computer
   D. none of the above

   2._____

3. A micro program is a collection of
   A. large scale operations
   B. DMA
   C. registers
   D. microinstructions

   3._____

4. The time a CPU takes to recognize an interrupt request is called
   A. interrupt latency
   B. timer delay
   B. response deadline
   D. throughput

   4._____

5. A _____ regulates the arrangement of the flow of microinstructions.
   A. multiplexer
   B. micro program controller
   C. DMA controller
   D. virtual memory

   5._____

6. Which of the following techniques will not be used when CPU exchanges data with a peripheral device?
   A. Interrupt driven I/O
   B. Direct Memory Access (DMA)
   C. Programmed I/O
   D. Virtual memory

   6._____

7. If a prior received character is not read by CPU and overwritten by new character received, the error will be called a _____ error.
   A. framing   B. parity   C. overrun   D. under-run

   7._____

8. Which of the following networks needs manual routing?
   A. Fiber optic   B. Bus   C. T-switched   D. Ring

   8._____

9. Which layer of TCP/IP responds to the OSI models to three layers?
   A. Application   B. Presentation   C. Session   D. Transport

   9._____

10. _____ transport layer protocols is connectionless.
    A. UDP   B. TCP   C. FTP   D. NVT

   10._____

11. _____ applications permit a user to approach and modify/change remote files without physical transfer.

    A. DNS   B. FTP   C. NFS   D. Telnet

11.____

12. Which of the following is a non-impact and quiet printer?

    A. Inkjet   B. Laser   C. Thermal   D. Dot matrix

12.____

13. Which of the following are high-end printers?

    A. Inkjet   B. Laser   C. Thermal   D. Dot matrix

13.____

14. For the purpose of plotting designs and graphs on papers, _____ is/are used.

    A. trackball   B. joystick   C. light pen   D. plotters

14.____

15. What is a Snowbol?

    A. Operating system   B. HLL

    C. Software   D. Search engine

15.____

16. Which of the following connects to a modem?

    A. Telephone line   B. Keyboard   C. Printer   D. Monitor

16.____

17. In automated organizations, _____ processing is used by large transaction processing systems.

    A. online   B. batch   C. once-a-day   D. end-of-day

17.____

18. What should a technician do after addition of a new cable segment to the network?

    A. Revise the disaster recovery plan

    B. Update the changes in document

    C. Update the wiring schematics

    D. None of the above

18.____

19. For the purpose of breaking up a broadcast domain, a _____ can be used.

    A. bridge   B. router

    C. DHCP server   D. printer

19.____

20. The secure way of transferring files between two devices is

    A. SFTP   B. SNMPv3   C. TFTP   D. FTP

20.____

21. An administrator networking closet (with all the networking and communication equipment) is on the second floor of a building and the communications lines are installed on the first floor. A _____ will be extended to connect communication lines to the networking closet.

    A. smart jack   B. demarcation point

    C. patch panel   D. router

21.____

22. To provide access to a VPN, _____ is used.

    A. IGP   B. PPTP   C. PPP   D. RAS

22.____

23. Two users are directly linked via RJ-45 and CAT5e cables and are communicating through IP. If the first user transmits data out of the RJ-45 on pins 1 and 2, the client should expect to receive a response on pins
    A. 1 and 2   B. 2 and 4   C. 3 and 6   D. 4 and 6

23.____

24. Examination of physical hardware addresses is done in _____ network access security method.
    A. IP filtering   B. L2TP   C. MAC filtering   D. RAS

24.____

25. Wireless standards give the direct advantage of
    A. increased use of wireless spectrum
    B. greater device security
    C. interoperability between devices
    D. increased number of protocols can be used

25.____

_____

KEY (CORRECT ANSWERS)

1.	A		11.	C	
2.	B		12.	A	
3.	D		13.	B	
4.	A		14.	D	
5.	B		15.	D	
6.	D		16.	A	
7.	C		17.	B	
8.	C		18.	C	
9.	A		19.	B	
10.	A		20.	A	

21.	C
22.	B
23.	C
24.	C
25.	C

_____

47

TEST 2

DIRECTIONS: Each question or incomplete statement is followed by several suggested answers or completions. Select the one that BEST answers the question or completes the statement. *PRINT THE LETTER OF THE CORRECT ANSWER IN THE SPACE AT THE RIGHT.*

1. What is an ALU?   1._____
   A. Arithmetic Logic Unit   B. Array Logic Unit
   C. Application Logic Unit   D. None of the above

2. In a client-server system, which type of computers are usually client   2._____
   computers?
   A. Mainframe   B. Mini computer
   C. Micro computer   D. PDA

3. A(n) _____ is necessary for a computer to *boot*.   3._____
   A. compiler   B. loader
   C. operating system   D. assembler

4. In the present technology age, computers are typically   4._____
   A. digital   B. analog   C. hybrid   D. complex

5. What is the physical structure of a computer called?   5._____
   A. CPU   B. Hardware   C. Software   D. All of the above

6. Data is represented in the form of discrete signals in a(n) _____ computer.   6._____
   A. analog   B. digital   C. both A and B D. hybrid

7. _____ is now available in the form of PC.   7._____
   A. Mainframe   B. Micro computer
   C. Mini computer   D. Both B and C

8. Which of the following is larger than a portable computer but is a small   8._____
   general function micro computer?
   A. Hybrid   B. Digital
   C. Desktop   D. None of the above

9. Most of the processing in a computer takes place in   9._____
   A. memory   B. RAM   C. both A and B D. CPU

10. What does LAN stand for?   10._____
    A. Limited Area Network   B. Logical Area Network
    C. Local Area Network   D. Large Area Network

11. Which of the following defines the rules and procedures for regulating data   11._____
    transmission over the internet?
    A. IP address   B. Domains   C. Protocol   D. Gateway

12. Which of the following protocol is used by the intranets, extranets and internet?
    A. TCP/IP   B. Protocol
    C. Open system   D. Internet work processor

12.____

13. On which ring does the data travel in FDDI?
    A. The primary   B. The secondary
    C. Both rings   D. None of the above

13.____

14. _____ is the logical topology.
    A. Bus   B. Tree   C. Star   D. Both A and C

14.____

15. The main drawback of ring topology is that
    A. if one computer fails, it affects the whole network
    B. adding/removing computers affects the network activity
    C. failure of the central hub makes the whole network unable to work
    D. both A and B

15.____

16. _____ is NOT anti-virus software.
    A. NAV   B. F-Prot   C. Oracle   D. McAfee

16.____

17. DMA stands for
    A. Direct Memory Allocation   B. Direct Memory Access
    C. Direct Module Access   D. none of the above

17.____

18. Which of the following is a storage device?
    A. Tape   B. Hard disk
    C. Floppy disk   D. All of the above

18.____

19. Which of the following are determined by user needs?
    A. System software   B. Application software
    C. Assemblers   D. Compilers

19.____

20. Which tools are available with system analysis?
    A. Review of procedure and conducting interviews
    B. Review of documentation and observation of the situation
    C. Conducting interviews and questionnaire administration
    D. Both B and C

20.____

21. Programs used to catch errors and their causes are called
    A. operating system extensions   B. cookies
    C. diagnostic software   D. boot diskettes

21.____

22. A virus which reproduces itself by using the computer host is called
    A. time bomb   B. worm
    C. Melissa virus   D. macro virus

22.____

23. The best practice for implementing a basic wireless network is
    A. disabling ESSID broadcast
    B. adding two access points per area of service
    C. not configuring the ESSID point
    D. none of the above

23._____

24. For connecting a single network node to a switch, _____ wiring standards will usually be used.
    A. loopback   B. straight   C. rollover   D. crossover

24._____

25. Before having a db loss, a CAT5 cable can run a maximum distance of
    A. 106 feet (31 meters)   B. 203 feet (60 meters)
    C. 328 feet (100 meters)   D. none of the above

25._____

———————

KEY (CORRECT ANSWERS)

1.	A		11.	C
2.	C		12.	A
3.	C		13.	A
4.	A		14.	C
5.	B		15.	D
6.	B		16.	C
7.	B		17.	B
8.	C		18.	D
9.	D		19.	A
10.	C		20.	D

21.	C
22.	B
23.	A
24.	B
25.	C

———————

TEST 3

DIRECTIONS: Each question or incomplete statement is followed by several suggested answers or completions. Select the one that BEST answers the question or completes the statement. *PRINT THE LETTER OF THE CORRECT ANSWER IN THE SPACE AT THE RIGHT.*

1. I/O port is an interface that is used to connect microcomputer bus to
   A. flip flops
   B. memory
   C. peripheral devices
   D. multiplexers

   1.____

2. In _____, a CPU poll after detecting an interrupt, determines the interrupting module and branches in an interrupt service routine.
   A. daisy chain
   B. software poll
   C. multiple interrupts lines
   D. all of the above

   2.____

3. Where is a separate address space for an I/O operation reserved for a CPU?
   A. Isolated I/O
   B. Memory mapped I/O
   C. Memory
   D. None of the above

   3.____

4. In _____ for resolving the priority, the highest priority device is placed at the first position followed by less priority devices.
   A. asynchronous methods
   B. daisy-chaining priority methods
   C. parallel method
   D. semi-synchronous method

   4.____

5. In _____, a part of the CPU's address lines constructing an input to the address decoder is neglected.
   A. microprogramming
   B. instruction pre-fetching
   C. pipelining
   D. partial decoding

   5.____

6. What is the data unit in TCP/IP called?
   A. Message   B. Segment   C. Datagram   D. Frame

   6.____

7. If a host domain name is known, what can DNS obtain?
   A. Station address
   B. IP address
   C. Port address
   D. Checksum

   7.____

8. _____ OSI layers correspond to TCP/IP's application layer.
   A. Application
   B. Presentation
   C. Session
   D. All of the above

   8.____

9. Devices on different networks can communicate with each other via a
   A. file server
   B. gateway
   C. printer server
   D. none of the above

   9.____

10. Which of the following can combine transmissions from different input/output devices into one line?
    A. Concentrator communication device
    B. Modifier
    C. Multiplexer
    D. Full duplex line

10.____

11. For the analysis of retinal scans, fingerprints, etc. in security access systems, which of the following techniques is used?
    A. Biometrics
    B. Bio measurement
    C. Computer security
    D. Smart weapon machinery

11.____

12. _____ guards a computer against unauthorized access to a network.
    A. Hacker-proof antivirus
    B. Firewall
    C. Encryption safe wall
    D. All of the above

12.____

13. What is scrambling of code called?
    A. Encryption
    B. Firewall
    C. Scrambling
    D. Password proofing

13.____

14. What should be used to prevent data loss due to power failure?
    A. Encryption program
    B. Surge protector
    C. Firewall
    D. UPS

14.____

15. If an administrator wants to install a device which can detect and control peer-to-peer traffic, a _____ device type will be installed.
    A. bandwidth shaper
    B. intrusion detection
    C. proxy server
    D. load balancer

15.____

16. If a technician needs to troubleshoot an unfamiliar network, the first step taken to diagnose the problem would be to
    A. report the problem to administrative technician
    B. make use of a port analyzer to analyze the network topology
    C. analyze symptoms and draw a network diagram
    D. all of the above

16.____

17. To discover MAC address of a connecting router, _____ commands can be used.
    A. ARP
    B. trace route
    C. ping
    D. ping sweep

17.____

18. E-mails sent to users with malicious website links are an example of
    A. viruses
    B. phishing
    C. rogue access points
    D. man-in-the-middle

18.____

19. To analyze that a RJ-45 jack in a cubicle responds to a specific RJ-45 jack in a patch panel, an administrator will use a
    A. punch-down tool
    B. spectrum analyzer
    C. toner probe
    D. multi-meter

19.____

20. _____ network types are suitable for a 10 gigabyte core network using 33 feet (10 meter) fiber runs.
   A. 10Base-FX
   B. 10GBase-SR
   C. 10GBase-SW
   D. None of the above
   20.____

21. When an administrator troubleshoots network connectivity and wants to view which packets are going through from workstation X to server 1, he will use _____ command line tools.
   A. view route
   B. route
   C. trace route
   D. ping
   21.____

22. For the purpose of updating physical network diagrams, revising _____ is the most appropriate policy.
   A. whenever a connection is changed
   B. before regularly scheduled network audits
   C. after new personnel are hired
   D. after weekly network support team review
   22.____

23. When a firewall accepts a request packet on port 80, it allows the reply packet to pass through automatically. This behavior of firewall is best described as
   A. stateful inspection
   B. intrusion detection
   C. content filtering
   D. passive fingerprinting
   23.____

24. A network technician can face _____ connectivity issues as a result of bundling network cables tightly together.
   A. collision
   B. attenuation
   C. crosstalk
   D. open circuit
   24.____

25. On a wireless network, a _____ mechanism uses a separate network authentication server.
   A. Kerberos
   B. TKIP
   C. RADIUS
   D. WEP
   25.____

KEY (CORRECT ANSWERS)

1.	C		11.	A
2.	B		12.	B
3.	A		13.	A
4.	C		14.	D
5.	D		15.	A
6.	D		16.	C
7.	B		17.	A
8.	D		18.	B
9.	B		19.	D
10.	C		20.	B

21.	C
22.	A
23.	A
24.	C
25.	C

TEST 4

DIRECTIONS: Each question or incomplete statement is followed by several suggested answers or completions. Select the one that BEST answers the question or completes the statement. *PRINT THE LETTER OF THE CORRECT ANSWER IN THE SPACE AT THE RIGHT.*

1. The electrical pathway through which the processor communicates with peripheral devices is called the
   A. computer bus   B. hazard   C. memory   D. disk

   1.____

2. If a 0 is transmitted instead of a stop bit, a(n) _____ error will be the serial communication error condition.
   A. framing   B. parity   C. overrun   D. under-run

   2.____

3. An interrupt can be defined as a process where
   A. an external device can speed up the working of the microprocessor
   B. input devices can take over the working of the microprocessor
   C. an external device gets the attention of the microprocessor
   D. none of the above

   3.____

4. What controls the sequence of the flow of microinstructions?
   A. Multiplexer   B. Micro program controller
   C. DMA controller   D. Virtual memory

   4.____

5. What is MSI?
   A. Medium Scale Integrated Circuits
   B. Medium System Intelligence
   C. Medium Scale Intelligent Circuit
   D. None of the above

   5.____

6. If a network has N number of devices and every device has N-1 ports for cables, this topology is known as
   A. mesh   B. star   C. bus   D. ring

   6.____

7. Usenet is also known as
   A. Gopher   B. Newsgroups   C. Browser   D. CERN

   7.____

8. Junk e-mail is also known as
   A. spam   B. spoof   C. sniffer script   D. spool

   8.____

9. Geographical scattered office LANS can be connected by
   A. VAN   B. LAN   C. DAN   D. WAN

   9.____

10. _____ gathers information of the user and sends it to someone over the internet.
    A. A virus   B. Spybot
    C. Logic bomb   D. Security patch

    10.____

11. A worm virus is terminated eventually due to the lack of   11._____
    A. memory or disk space   B. time
    C. CD drive space   D. CD-RW

12. Instructions of a computer are executed by direct involvement of the   12._____
    A. scanner   B. main storage
    C. secondary storage   D. processor

13. Most processing of a computer takes place in   13._____
    A. memory   B. RAM   C. motherboard   D. CPU

14. Which of the following is NOT a storage medium?   14._____
    A. Hard disk   B. Flash drive   C. DVD   D. Scanner

15. Suppose a user calls you for network support and says that his e-mail is not   15._____
working. What will you do first?
    A. Inquire about the operation performed by the user and what was the
       expected and actual result
    B. Restart the hub the user was connected to
    C. Send a test e-mail message to see if it's sent
    D. None of the above

16. Suppose two networks in different departments are using DHCP set up for   16._____
192.168.0.0/24 and after consolidation of the officer's network we have run out
of IP addresses. The BEST cost-effective solution for this will be
    A. adding a router to connect both networks
    B. switching to static IP addressing
    C. changing the subnet mask to 255.255.254.0
    D. none of the above

17. Suppose that packets to an IP address are getting lost over the internet.   17._____
Which tools will an administrator use to find out the responsible hop?
    A. Ping   B. nslookup   C. Trace route   D. netstat

18. What should a technician check if a workstation on the network is able to   18._____
ping hosts on the network but it is not able to ping any addresses on the
internet?
    A. The DNS server entries   B. The network card
    C. The default gateway   D. The host's file

19. To find out the status of all established TCP connections by port 80, the   19._____
administrator will use the _____ command.
    A. netstat –at   B. netstat –r   C. netstat –v   D. netstat -p tcp

20. To evaluate the network traffic, which of the following tools will be used?   20._____
    A. OTDR   B. Protocol analyzer
    C. Certifier   D. Toner probe

21. Which port is usually used for FTP traffic?   21.____
    A. 20   B. 22   C. 23   D. 25

22. _____ can function as a router, support VLANs and connect multiple   22.____
    workstations.
    A. Repeater   B. Switch
    C. Hub   D. Multilayer switch

23. 208.177.23.1 belongs to class   23.____
    A. A   B. B   C. C   D. D

24. If 25 clients on the same network want to see a video, _____ should be   24.____
    configured on the user's computer to reduce network traffic.
    A. class C addresses   B. class A addresses
    C. broadcast   D. multicast

25. Suppose we have installed a new LAN switch on fiber ports. In order to   25.____
    allow compatibility to the existing fiber network, what will a technician need on
    the new switch?
    A. Router   B. Repeater
    C. Media converter   D. Hub

KEY (CORRECT ANSWERS)

1.	A		11.	A
2.	A		12.	D
3.	C		13.	D
4.	B		14.	D
5.	A		15.	A
6.	A		16.	C
7.	B		17.	C
8.	A		18.	C
9.	D		19.	D
10.	B		20.	B

21.	A
22.	D
23.	C
24.	D
25.	C

EXAMINATION SECTION

TEST 1

DIRECTIONS: Each question or incomplete statement is followed by several suggested answers or completions. Select the one that BEST answers the question or completes the statement. *PRINT THE LETTER OF THE CORRECT ANSWER IN THE SPACE AT THE RIGHT.*

1. Modern day telephony uses _____ for sending voice signals.　　　　　　　　1._____
   A. VoIP   B. modems   C. routers   D. switches

2. A user is downloading a file using a computer on the network. The computer is a(n)　　2._____
   A. node   B. entry point   C. client   D. access point

3. A network operating system offers its services to　　　　　　　　　　　　3._____
   A. groups of computers using desktop operating system
   B. groups of servers connected to LAN
   C. users in another network segment
   D. all of the above

4. The program to interpret HTML files sent from a web server is called　　　　　4._____
   A. browser   B. SMTP server
   C. RAS   D. HTML engine

5. FrameRelay is used in　　　　　　　　　　　　　　　　　　　　　　　5._____
   A. LAN   B. MAN   C. WAN   D. PAN

6. The most secure network is　　　　　　　　　　　　　　　　　　　　6._____
   A. LAN   B. MAN   C. WAN   D. PAN

7. In a _____ network, any computer could be a client or server.　　　　　　　7._____
   A. peer-to-peer   B. client server
   B. VLAN   D. terrestrial

8. User documents have been stored on a central server for printing. This is an　　8._____
   example of a(n) _____ server.
   A. application   B. file   C. print   D. mail

9. Small computer programs are being run from a central computer. This is　　　9._____
   a(n) _____ kind of server.
   A. application   B. file   c. print   D. mail

10. Databases are stored in a(n) _____ server.　　　　　　　　　　　　　10._____
    A. database   B. file   C. data   D. information

11. Data resources are placed at different geographical locations, however, they　　11._____
    are managed from one unique location. What kind of network model is this?
    A. Centralized   B. Remote   C. Distributed   D. Isolated

12. A company has a private network used within its premises. It has given access to a few outside suppliers through its

    A. intranet   B. extranet   C. internet   D. subnet

12.____

13. You are using your browser to browse a web page using HTTP protocol. _____ protocol will be used to respond to your request.

    A. HTTP   B. TCP   C. HTTPS   D. IP

13.____

14. _____ protocols are not specific to one supplier of LAN equipment.

    A. Proprietary   B. Functional   C. Universal   D. Standard

14.____

15. RFCs are used to upgrade the bandwidth requirements of a protocol. RFC stands for

    A. Requirement for Formal Consent   B. Regional Formats Committee
    C. Request For Comments   D. Released Future Concerns

15.____

16. LAN standards for networking are developed by _____ organization.

    A. IERT   B. IEEE   C. FERS   D. OOEE

16.____

17. Standard allocation of Internet protocol addresses are insured by an organization called

    A. ICANN   B. Internet Architecture Board (IAB)
    C. IEEE   D. Internet Society

17.____

18. A network switch is connected to 15 employees. _____ topology is in use.

    A. Star   B. Bus   C. Ring   D. Hybrid

18.____

19. _____ optic fiber cable will be used for smaller distances.

    A. Single Mode Fiber (SMF)   B. Multi-Mode Fiber (MMF)
    C. Both A and B   D. None of the above

19.____

20. The entire bandwidth of a digital signal is being used by the only channel. It is called a(n) _____ communication.

    A. broadband   B. digital   C. analog   D. baseband

20.____

21. Frequency Division Multiplexing (FDM) is possible in

    A. baseband   B. broadband
    C. both A and B   D. none of the above

21.____

22. Gigabit Ethernet is capable of transmissions of 1000

    A. BPS   B. GBPS   C. MBPS   D. KBPS

22.____

23. Fiber distributed data interface uses _____ topology.

    A. ring   B. star   C. mesh   D. bus

23.____

24. IEEE networking standards apply to the _____ layer specifications technology.

    A. network   B. data   C. application   D. physical

24.____

25. Mutual authentication between the client and the server is called   25.____
    A. encrypted
    B. decrypted
    C. challenge handshake
    D. kerberos

KEY (CORRECT ANSWERS)

1.	A		11.	C
2.	C		12.	B
3.	D		13.	A
4.	A		14.	D
5.	C		15.	C
6.	A		16.	B
7.	A		17.	A
8.	B		18.	A
9.	A		19.	A
10.	A		20.	D

21.	B
22.	C
23.	A
24.	A
25.	A

TEST 2

DIRECTIONS: Each question or incomplete statement is followed by several suggested answers or completions. Select the one that BEST answers the question or completes the statement. *PRINT THE LETTER OF THE CORRECT ANSWER IN THE SPACE AT THE RIGHT.*

1. Fast Ethernet can run on   1._____
    A. UTP   B. optical fiber
    C. wireless   D. all of the above

2. Fiber fast Ethernet can provide speeds of up to   2._____
    A. 1 GBPS   B. 512 MBPS   C. 100 MBPS   D. 256 KBPS

3. Giga-Ethernet provides speed up to _____ MBPS over fiber.   3._____
    A. 1000   B. 512   C. 256   D. 1.5

4. _____ LAN is a solution to divide a single broadcast domain into multiple 4._____
    broadcast domains.
    A. Virtual   B. Localized   C. Bridged   D. Broadcast

5. Internet uses _____ topology.   5._____
    A. hybrid   B. daisy chain C. dual ring   D. mesh

6. Unlike OSI, the Internet model uses _____ layers.   6._____
    A. 3   B. 4   C. 7   D. 5

7. Infrared frequency ranges from 300 GHz to 43 THz and is used for   7._____
    A. TV remotes
    B. penetrating obstacles
    C. communications of up to 1000 meters
    D. line of sight communication

8. Frequency Division Multiplexing (FDM) uses _____ to distribute bandwidth. 8._____
    A. frequency   B. channels   C. time slots D. path

9. _____ is used to provide abstraction of services.   9._____
    A. Abstraction layer   B. Network layer
    C. Encapsulation   D. Collision detection

10. _____ are addressed via ports.   10._____
    A. Processes   B. Memory address
    C. NIC   D. Protocols

11. SMTP is _____-level protocol.
    A. higher   B. lower   C. user   D. network
    11._____

12. _____ layer provides host-to-host communications.
    A. Network   B. Data   C. Transport   D. Physical
    12._____

13. _____ is basic transport layer protocol.
    A. UDP   B. HTTP   C. HTTPS   D. FTP
    13._____

14. Adding a packet header is a function of
    A. transport   B. physical   C. data link   D. application
    14._____

15. _____ requires sending from one network to another.
    A. Internetworking   B. Transmission control
    C. TCP   D. IP
    15._____

16. A host is identified using
    A. IP addressing system   B. website address
    C. MAC address   D. Checksum
    16._____

17. 128-bit addressing is made possible by
    A. IPV4   B. IPV6   C. TCP/IP   D. UDP
    17._____

18. HDLC stands for
    A. High Level Link Control   B. High Level Data Level Checking
    C. High Definition Latency Check   D. High Definition Least Control
    18._____

19. IP (Internet Protocol) does NOT guarantee _____ delivery.
    A. reliable   B. efficient   C. error-free   D. complete
    19._____

20. Routers and _____ do not examine traffic.
    A. graphic cards   B. bridges
    C. network hubs   d switches
    20._____

21. A PAN may use _____ protocol.
    A. Bluetooth   B. IP   C. TCP   D. UDP
    21._____

22. A wireless router typically allows devices to connect to
    A. a wired network
    B. a wireless network
    C. both wired and wireless networks
    D. predefined devices on other networks
    22._____

23. _____ may refer to a Wi-Fi use without permission.
    A. Piggybacking   B. Address breach
    C. Access point hack   D. IP address violation
    23._____

24. FTTN in fiber networks denotes Fiber
    A. Technology Tracking Network
    C. Transmission Twisted Network
    B. to the Neighborhood
    D. Traceability Track Nationwide

24.____

25. PON stands for _____ Network.
    A. Passive Optic
    C. Privately Owned
    B. Private Optic
    D. Primary Operational

25.____

KEY (CORRECT ANSWERS)

1.	D		11.	A
2.	C		12.	C
3.	A		13.	A
4.	A		14.	C
5.	A		15.	A
6.	B		16.	A
7.	A		17.	B
8.	B		18.	A
9.	C		19.	A
10.	A		20.	D

21.	A
22.	C
23.	A
24.	B
25.	A

TEST 3

DIRECTIONS: Each question or incomplete statement is followed by several suggested answers or completions. Select the one that BEST answers the question or completes the statement. *PRINT THE LETTER OF THE CORRECT ANSWER IN THE SPACE AT THE RIGHT.*

1. MIMO stands for
   A. Multiple Input Multiple Output
   B. Multiple Inter Modular Operations
   C. Metropolitan Inter Module Onset
   D. Metropolitan Intra Modular Offnet

   1._____

2. Beamforming characterizes
   A. merging of optic fiber streams
   B. merging of signals
   C. line of sight light beams
   D. unidirectional radio streams

   2._____

3. Speed of transmission will be SLOWEST in
   A. LAN   B. WAN   C. MAN   D. PAN

   3._____

4. Network Interface Cards (NIC) use a(n) _____ to distinguish one computer from another.
   A. network address
   B. IP address
   C. MAC address
   D. Checksum

   4._____

5. Which of the following amplify communication signals and filter noise?
   A. Hubs   B. Switches   C. Routers   D. Repeaters

   5._____

6. _____ send information/data to be copied unmodified to all computers.
   A. Hubs   B. Bridges   C. Firewalls   D. Switches

   6._____

7. Which of the following reject network access requests from unsafe sources?
   A. Filter services
   B. Hubs
   C. Security protocols
   D. Firewalls

   7._____

8. A _____ normally represents the smallest amount of data that can traverse over a network at a single time.
   A. byte   B. bit   C. word   D. packet

   8._____

9. OSPF is a
   A. routing protocol
   B. unique addressing scheme
   C. end user identification technique
   D. open source software

   9._____

10. _____ route is used when failure occurs with a routing device.
    A. Adaptive   B. Alternate   C. Access   D. Appropriate

    10._____

11. _____ is a parameter used for calculating a routing metric.
    A. Path speed   B. Load   C. Hop count   D. All of the above

    11._____

12. Algorithm in computer operations is a   12._____
    A. software   B. hardware   C. method   D. pseudo code

13. _____ is the total time a packet takes to transmit from one place to another.   13._____
    A. Response time   B. Latency
    C. Delay   D. Bandwidth

14. Media portion in an OSI model includes   14._____
    A. presentation and data layer
    B. application and network layer
    C. transport and data layer
    D. all of the network data link and physical layers

15. OSI stands for Open   15._____
    A. Systems Interconnection   B. Standards International
    C. Systems Integration   D. Standards for Internet

16. Collision occurs when   16._____
    A. packets collide due to throttling
    B. more than one computer sends data at the same time
    C. data is sent out of sequence
    D. network traffic exceeds its limit

17. CSMA is a method used by   17._____
    A. Ethernet   B. Internet
    C. operating system   D. error detection services

18. The term broadband is used when a media type   18._____
    A. can carry multiple data signals
    B. can carry one signal at one time
    C. has separate lines for sending and receiving
    D. has error detection and correction mechanism

19. Fast Ethernet is also known as   19._____
    A. 10 Base-T   B. 100 Base-T
    C. Gigabit Ethernet   D. 1000 Base-X

20. _____ is called beacon frame.   20._____
    A. Periodically broadcasted frame   B. Identification frame
    C. Header frame   D. Frame beginning the broadcast

21. Channel bonding allows multiple _____ at the same time.   21._____
    A. packets   B. channels   C. media   D. data streams

22. Gigabit Ethernet works on _____ media.   22._____
    A. fiber optic   B. copper
    C. both fiber and copper   D. wireless

23. FDDI uses _____ rings.
    A. four   B. two   C. one   D. three   23.____

24. IPV6 addresses are _____ bits.
    A. 32   B. 65   C. 128   D. 256   24.____

25. IPV6 addresses are binary numbers represented in
    A. decimal   B. binary   C. octal   D. hexadecimal   25.____

KEY (CORRECT ANSWERS)

1.	A		11.	D
2.	D		12.	C
3.	C		13.	B
4.	C		14.	D
5.	D		15.	A
6.	A		16.	B
7.	D		17.	A
8.	D		18.	A
9.	A		19.	B
10.	A		20.	A

21.	B
22.	C
23.	B
24.	C
25.	D

TEST 4

DIRECTIONS: Each question or incomplete statement is followed by several suggested answers or completions. Select the one that BEST answers the question or completes the statement. *PRINT THE LETTER OF THE CORRECT ANSWER IN THE SPACE AT THE RIGHT.*

1. VoIP allows sending voice data using
   A. fiber optics
   B. PSTN
   C. standard IP
   D. copper wires

   1._____

2. Bootstrapping refers to the _____ process.
   A. self-starting
   B. batch processing
   C. infinite
   D. automatically ending

   2._____

3. NOS stands for Network
   A. Operation Starter
   B. On Standby
   C. Optic Stream
   D. Operating System

   3._____

4. Compared to LANs, WANS are more
   A. reliable   B. congested   C. error-free   D. cheaper

   4._____

5. The initial setup costs for LAN are _____ compared to WAN.
   A. the same   B. low   C. high   D. very high

   5._____

6. WANs are often built using
   A. more than one adjacent LAN
   B. leased lines
   C. fiber optic cables
   D. extranet

   6._____

7. The operating and maintenance costs of WAN are _____ compared to LAN.
   A. very low   B. low   C. high   D. very high

   7._____

8. Nowadays, most LAN(s) use _____ as standard.
   A. Ethernet
   B. VPN over Internet
   C. frame relay
   D. leased lines

   8._____

9. WANs may use _____ as standard.
   A. Ethernet
   B. Subnet
   C. VPN
   D. Fast Ethernet

   9._____

10. A computer network spanning three university campuses within remote geographical locations is a typical example of a _____ area network.
    A. campus   B. wide   C. metropolitan   D. local

    10._____

11. Client server networks require a _____ server.
    A. dedicated   B. parallel   C. data   D. file

    11._____

12. A file server will typically run _____ protocol.
    A. HTTP   B. IP   C. HTTPs   D. FTP

    12._____

13. _____ servers allow central administration of user and network resources.   13.____
    A. Print   B. Directory   C. File   D. Application

14. Network resources will be optimally used from a central resource in a   14.____
    _____ computer network model.
    A. central   B. distributed   C. remote   D. wireless

15. An internetwork will connect at least two   15.____
    A. internets   B. extranets   C. intranets   D. networks

16. Internet Protocol Security (IPSec) is a(n) _____ part of the IPV4.   16.____
    A. optional   B. integral/mandatory
    C. built-in   D. missing

17. Features of _____ can be extended by adding headers.   17.____
    A. IPV4   B. IPV6   C. IP   D. TCP

18. The available types of communication in IPV4 are unicast, multicast and   18.____
    A. podcast   B. broadcast   C. lancast   D. delicast

19. In backup terminology, a cold site means   19.____
    A. needs time to switch to normal operations
    B. readily available backup
    C. a backup on Cloud
    D. a separate backup

20. An overlapping frame is called a(n)   20.____
    A. header   B. packet
    C. collision   D. extended frame

21. _____ is a set of checks/rules for communication.   21.____
    A. Protocol   B. Syntax
    C. Lexical grammar   D. Encryption

22. Multiplexing collects data from different   22.____
    A. networks   B. applications C. addresses   D. routers

23. When a block of data is transmitted, supplement data is attached to the   23.____
    _____ for use from one layer to another.
    A. datagram   B. packet   C. FIN bit   D. header

24. De-multiplexing is done in a(n) _____ layer.   24.____
    A. transport   B. network   C. data   D. application

25. In large networks, a _____ will divide the network into logical parts called 25.____
    segments to handle data traffic.
    A. switch   B. hub   C. router   D. bridge

KEY (CORRECT ANSWERS)

1.	C		11.	A
2.	A		12.	D
3.	D		13.	C
4.	B		14.	A
5.	B		15.	D
6.	B		16.	B
7.	C		17.	B
8.	A		18.	B
9.	C		19.	A
10.	C		20.	C

21.	A
22.	B
23.	D
24.	A
25.	C

EXAMINATION SECTION

TEST 1

DIRECTIONS: Each question or incomplete statement is followed by several suggested answers or completions. Select the one that BEST answers the question or completes the statement. *PRINT THE LETTER OF THE CORRECT ANSWER IN THE SPACE AT THE RIGHT.*

1.   _____ computer(s) can transmit data at a time in a network.   1._____
    A. Sender and the receiver   B. Only one
    C. All   D. Selected

2.   Switching networks are also called _____ networks.   2._____
    A. streaming   B. transmission   C. packet   D. routing

3.   Data may be lost in transmission. _____ will help the transmitter and   3._____
    receiver to determine correctly received data.
    A. Fair use   B. Coordination
    C. Packet layers   D. Correction bit

4.   A network has a capacity of 3 minutes to transfer a file of 3 MB. Therefore,   4._____
    A. a 3 MB file is always transferred in 3 minutes
    B. priority transfer time is 3 minutes for a 3 MB file
    C. network congestion is no more than 3 minutes
    D. wait time for each new transfer is 3 minutes

5.   While a 3 MB file is being transmitted, a 3 KB file is added for transmission.   5._____
    A. 3 MB file will be sent in the same time as previous
    B. 3 MB file is delayed
    C. 3 KB file is delayed
    D. There is no effect on transmission time

6.   All packets enter the transmission medium at   6._____
    A. demultiplexor   B. multiplexor   C. hub   D. switch

7.   Packet size   7._____
    A. must be standard for all hardware technologies
    B. targets the format of the frame used
    C. varies with the hardware used
    D. depends on the type of transmission medium

8.   Frame has a   8._____
    A. begin bit and end bit   B. start and stop bit
    C. header and trailer   D. predetermined size

9. Sending computer will transmit frame in this sequence:
   A. End (EOT), Header (SOH), Data
   B. Data and End (EOT)
   C. End (EOT), Data and Header (SOH)
   D. Header (SOH), Data and End (EOT)

   9.____

10. EOT is missing. This indicates
    A. the sender crashed   B. the receiver malfunctioned
    C. the packet was discarded   D. transmission medium is faulty

    10.____

11. A bad frame is detected. It will be
    A. resent   B. corrected with a parity bit
    C. discarded   D. transmitted with error bit

    11.____

12. _____ is a technique to encode reserved bytes.
    A. Bit stuffing   B. Encryption
    C. Modulation   D. Encapsulation

    12.____

13. _____ makes a pair of bytes from Reserved Byte.
    A. Receiver   B. Sender
    C. Buffering algorithm   D. Packet

    13.____

14. Unwanted data is generated due to
    A. transmission errors   B. incorrect frame format
    C. parity bit   D. byte stuffing

    14.____

15. Incorrect data is rejected during
    A. error correction   B. demultiplexing
    C. multiplexing   D. error detection

    15.____

16. In 11100011, parity is
    A. even   B. odd   C. biased   D. checksum

    16.____

17. One of the bits is changed from 0 to 1. The parity of resulting bits
    A. becomes undefined   B. is wrong
    C. always changes to 0   D. always changes to 1

    17.____

18. _____ detects erroneous data.
    A. Sender after receiving error bit   B. Error correction algorithm
    C. Packet   D. Receiver based on parity

    18.____

19. _____ is an error detection technique.
    A. CRC   B. CSMA   C. Byte stuffing   D. CMC

    19.____

20. Checksum uses
    A. parity   B. redundancy   C. collision   D. sum of data

    20.____

21. Unrolling loop is an _____ technique.
    A. optimization
    B. error detection
    C. error correction
    D. error

21.____

22. CRC stands for
    A. Core Recall Cycle
    B. Critical Recycle Code
    C. Coded Redundancy Check
    D. Cyclic Redundancy Check

22.____

23. CRC will follow
    A. SOH
    B. EOT
    C. parity bit
    D. error frame

23.____

24. In shared networks, data reaches _____ destination(s).
    A. selected
    B. all
    C. nearest node
    D. none of the above

24.____

25. Each station has a unique _____ address.
    A. frame
    B. hardware
    C. generic
    D. operational

25.____

KEY (CORRECT ANSWERS)

1.	B		11.	C
2.	C		12.	A
3.	B		13.	B
4.	D		14.	A
5.	A		15.	D
6.	B		16.	B
7.	C		17.	B
8.	C		18.	D
9.	D		19.	A
10.	A		20.	D

21.	A
22.	D
23.	B
24.	B
25.	B

TEST 2

DIRECTIONS: Each question or incomplete statement is followed by several suggested answers or completions. Select the one that BEST answers the question or completes the statement. *PRINT THE LETTER OF THE CORRECT ANSWER IN THE SPACE AT THE RIGHT.*

1.   _____ adds hardware address to outgoing frames.   1.____
      A. Byte stuffing   B. CSMA   C. DMA   D. LAN interface

2.   _____ defines access rules.   2.____
      A. DMA   B. CD/CSMA   C. Parity bit   D. Bit stuffing

3.   Each time a packet passes through the router, the number of _____   3.____
      increases by 1.
      A. address bytes   B. hops
      C. subnet masks   D. processing cycles

4.   The hardware address is typically one to _____ bytes.   4.____
      A. four   B. eight   C. sixteen   D. six

5.   _____ address is used to send messages to all stations.   5.____
      A. Broadcast   B. Abstract   C. Podcast   D. Unique

6.   The data area following the header is called   6.____
      A. payload   B. frame   C. loader info   D. packet

7.   An interface which receives all frames for analysis is   7.____
      A. DMA   B. promiscuous mode
      C. NIC   D. CSMA

8.   Analyzer can display real time info by   8.____
      A. capturing specific frames   B. computing totals
      C. counting frames   D. analyzing parity bits

9.   _____ can be used over a long distance.   9.____
      A. RS-232   B. Oscillating signal carriers
      C. Encoded signaling   D. Beacon

10.   Carrier modulation can be used with _____ medium.   10.____
      A. fiber   B. copper   C. radio   D. all types of

11.   _____ modulation involves timing shifts.   11.____
      A. Amplitude   B. Frequency   C. Phase shift   D. TDM

12.   _____ is the responsibility of the modulator.   12.____
      A. Encoding of the data bits   B. Decoding of data bits
      C. Transmission of the data   D. Error detection in carrier

13. Simultaneous _____ communication requires a modulator as well as a demodulator.
    A. half duplex   B. full duplex
    C. asynchronous   D. modulated
    13._____

14. Transducers using modulation through sound use
    A. glass   B. dial-up   C. radio   D. copper
    14._____

15. Air carries multiple signals called _____ for each TV station.
    A. frequency   B. amplitude   C. channels   D. modulations
    15._____

16. Switching data streams sequentially is
    A. TDM   B. FDM   C. DTM   D. DMA
    16._____

17. Network resources are managed using _____ service in Windows server-based networks.
    A. Windows active directory   B. Windows NT directory servicer
    C. NDM   D. DMS
    17._____

18. IP subnets connected using fast links are called
    A. domain   B. controller   C. site   D. BDC
    18._____

19. Object attributes in active directory are contained in
    A. configuration NC   B. CMD log
    C. MMC   D. Schema NC
    19._____

20. For group policy objects, a folder exists on all domain controllers as
    A. SYSVOL   B. C$ C. $SYS   D. \\shared
    20._____

21. A minimum required services and roles will run in
    A. minimal installation option   B. VMS
    C. server core   D. named piping
    21._____

22. Minimum storage required for active directory is
    A. 100 MB   B. 200 MB   C. 250 MB   D. 512 MB
    22._____

23. Administrators for duration of the schema update have the role of _____ Admins.
    A. Global   B. Schema   C. Security   D. Data
    23._____

24. A site created when installed in a forest root domain controller will derive its name from
    A. default first site name   B. default site built in
    C. $wins   D. NC
    24._____

25. A server that manages site-to-site replication is
    A. Bridgehead   B. Masthead   C. PDC   D. member
    25._____

KEY (CORRECT ANSWERS)

1.	D	11.	D
2.	B	12.	A
3.	B	13.	B
4.	D	14.	B
5.	A	15.	C
6.	A	16.	A
7.	B	17.	A
8.	B	18.	C
9.	B	19.	D
10.	D	20.	A

21.	C
22.	B
23.	B
24.	A
25.	A

TEST 3

DIRECTIONS: Each question or incomplete statement is followed by several suggested answers or completions. Select the one that BEST answers the question or completes the statement. *PRINT THE LETTER OF THE CORRECT ANSWER IN THE SPACE AT THE RIGHT.*

1. In Unix variants, _____ command is used to generate statistics on socket connections.
   A. SS   B. NETSTAT   C. IPNET   D. ST

   1._____

2. The _____ command is used to send mail via SMTP server.
   A. MAILX   B. SMAIL   C. NETSND   D. CONM

   2._____

3. Fdisk command on Linus is used to
   A. format hard disk   B. check partition
   C. copy contents   D. remove bad sectors

   3._____

4. The _____ command is used to open the command prompt in Windows.
   A. LST   B. PRM   C. TASKMGR   D. CMD

   4._____

5. IOS stands for
   A. Internet Operating System   B. Internetwork Operating System
   C. Internal Operating System   D. Input Output System

   5._____

6. Which is TRUE of a switch connected in a star topology?
   A. Packets are sent to all recipients in the network
   B. Packets are sent to intended recipients
   C. Packets are filtered by the recipient
   D. Packets are filtered by the sender

   6._____

7. Which is NOT an Ethernet cable standard?
   A. CAT-5   B. CAT-6   C. CAT-6e   D. CAT-5e

   7._____

8. Ethernet cables physically differ by
   A. quality of material used   B. number of twists per cm
   C. color coding scheme   D. number of wire pairs

   8._____

9. The term NEXT is used for
   A. lost packets   B. cable faults   C. parity   D. cross talk

   9._____

10. A stranded cable is
    A. an unused cable
    B. loosely connected
    C. made up of multiple cables
    D. the main cause of communication error

    10._____

11. Trusted Platform Module (TPM) is a(n)   11._____
    A. application software   B. hardware chip
    C. Ethernet cabling standard   D. encryption standard

12. Which statement is TRUE for BitLocker?   12._____
    A. It secures files one by one
    B. It secures the entire operating system
    C. It locks the entire drive
    D. It removes viruses

13. Web servers use _____ virtualization.   13._____
    A. server   B. desktop   C. application   D. data

14. _____ is a Linux OS.   14._____
    A. CMOS   B. VMS   C. Novell   D. Ubuntu

15. Wi-Fi means   15._____
    A. IEEE 802   B. wireless fidelity
    C. wireless first   D. SMPTE

16. _____ computing uses unused processing cycles from different computers.   16._____
    A. Cloud   B. Network   C. Packet   D. Grid

17. The _____ command will be used to change file permissions.   17._____
    A. CHKDSK   B. CHFLS   C. CHMOD   D. CHALP

18. CDFS is used for   18._____
    A. Window Active directory permissions
    B. making file system changes permanent
    C. checking for errors
    D. while reading CD-ROM

19. _____ is a technology provided for e-mail clients.   19._____
    A. Clutter   B. NOVA   C. ARPANET   D. Outlook

20. Unix users are protected by a firewall service named   20._____
    A. TCP wrapper   B. Fast TCP
    C. Modbus TCP/IP   D. TOE

21. _____ mode allows troubleshooting of Windows critical errors.   21._____
    A. Safe   B. Command line
    C. Line operation   D. CHKLST

22. Protocol _____ allows multiple protocols to work together.   22._____
    A. stack   B. pool   C. block   D. cloud

23. BCD is a data standard representing integers in _____ bits.   23._____
    A. 4   B. 8   C. 16   D. 32

24. Copying digital content from a device of one type to another is   24.____
    A. space shifting   B. CODEC
    C. openshift   D. proportional spacing

25. A zero that exists on the leftmost digit of a number is   25.____
    A. significant   B. absolute   C. rounding   D. leading

_____

KEY (CORRECT ANSWERS)

1.	A		11.	B
2.	A		12.	C
3.	B		13.	A
4.	D		14.	D
5.	B		15.	A
6.	B		16.	D
7.	B		17.	C
8.	B		18.	D
9.	D		19.	A
10.	C		20.	A

21.	A
22.	A
23.	A
24.	A
25.	D

_____

TEST 4

Each question or incomplete statement is followed by several suggested answers or completions. Select the one that BEST answers the question or completes the statement. *PRINT THE LETTER OF THE CORRECT ANSWER IN THE SPACE AT THE RIGHT.*

1. _____ interface allows a working based on body movements.   1._____
    A. Cyber   B. Nova   C. Rota   D. Haptic

2. Computers within the same domain acting as servers can have exactly   2._____
    _____ role(s).
    A. one   B. three   C. two   D. four

3. _____ is a part of an operating system.   3._____
    A. Kernel   B. Core   C. Grid   D. Cloud

4. File servers and application servers will typically be _____ servers in a   4._____
    Windows environment.
    A. data server   B. active directory
    C. cluster   D. member

5. Any of the network computers can be the server in _____ network.   5._____
    A. client server   B. VLAN   C. peer-to-peer   D. terrestrial

6. Ad-hoc mode does NOT use any   6._____
    A. shared services   B. access point
    C. protocol   D. data standards

7. Manchester encoding is a data _____ method.   7._____
    A. encryption   B. correction   C. compression   D. transmission

8. _____ server stores databases.   8._____
    A. File   B. Database   C. Data   D. Information

9. In a(n) _____ network, data may be coming from many sources but managed   9._____
    centrally.
    A. centralized   B. remote   C. distributed   D. isolated

10. Users outside of network are also allowed. They are part of the   10._____
    A. intranet   B. internet   C. subnet   D. extranet

11. Internet service providers are connected to each other using   11._____
    A. network access points (NAP)   B. access point (AP)
    C. APLink   D. virtual access points

12. An organization's network accessible to its staff only is a   12._____
    A. LAN   B. internet   C. intranet   D. WAN

13. _____ is memory area an application is legally allowed to access.
    A. Viber space   B. Address space
    C. Application memory   D. Physical memory

13.____

14. MAC OS always uses _____ addressing.
    A. segmented   B. thunking   C. flat   D. virtual

14.____

15. Multicast address is assigned to _____ device(s).
    A. one   B. any two specific
    C. NIC only   D. multiple

15.____

16. With _____, a packet can have multiple destinations.
    A. Mbone   B. MIDL   C. SDS   D. DDL

16.____

17. Rules and regulations governing the management of data are called
    A. computer law   B. compliance
    C. code law   D. GRC

17.____

18. An application in Windows that allows creating routing applications is
    A. RDMA   B. BRAS
    C. social routing   D. RRAS

18.____

19. A fiber-based distributed data interface will typically use _____ topology.
    A. star   B. mesh   C. bus   D. ring

19.____

20. The number of bits transferred from one device to another in 1 second is _____ rate.
    A. adaptive   B. bit   C. baud   D. passive

20.____

21. _____ is a scripting language used in Windows server OS, used for automating Windows management.
    A. Powershell   B. Vbscript   C. JDBC   D. JSON

21.____

22. What tool would you use for writing snap-ins in Windows?
    A. Powershell   B. WHS console
    C. APM   D. MMC

22.____

23. _____ monitors the packet collision rate.
    A. NIC   B. Switch   C. Router   D. API

23.____

24. Dynamic packet filtering is a feature of _____ architecture.
    A. firewall   B. DNA   C. FDDI   D. service

24.____

25. WHS denotes Windows
    A. hash system   B. home server
    C. hypertext service   D. help service

25.____

KEY (CORRECT ANSWERS)

1.	D		11.	B
2.	C		12.	C
3.	A		13.	B
4.	D		14.	C
5.	C		15.	D
6.	B		16.	A
7.	D		17.	B
8.	B		18.	D
9.	C		19.	D
10.	D		20.	B

21.	A
22.	D
23.	C
24.	A
25.	B

EXAMINATION SECTION

TEST 1

DIRECTIONS: Each question or incomplete statement is followed by several suggested answers or completions. Select the one that BEST answers the question or completes the statement. *PRINT THE LETTER OF THE CORRECT ANSWER IN THE SPACE AT THE RIGHT.*

1. The term that is used to refer to the storage and retrieval of data is
   A. website   B. database   C. software   D. application

   1._____

2. If you need to store employee data with all the information about the employees, you will store it in a
   A. relation   B. tuple   C. attribute   D. entity

   2._____

3. The term used to describe a specific property of a record is
   A. tuple   B. attribute   C. column   D. row

   3._____

4. Which of the following is used to reflect that records are unique?
   A. Foreign key   B. Candidate key
   C. Primary key   D. Index

   4._____

5. Database can be represented by _____ diagram.
   A. database   B. entity relationship
   C. data flow   D. all of the above

   5._____

6. You can create a table with the statement of _____ table.
   A. create   B. make   C. add   D. define

   6._____

7. A hierarchy representing super type/sub type may have which of the following properties?
   A. One super type may only have one sub type
   B. One sub type may have only one super type
   C. Each sub type may only have one attribute
   D. All of the above

   7._____

8. In the first normal form, the data must be represented by
   A. a primary key
   B. a single value in each cell of the table
   C. more than one table
   D. all of the above

   8._____

9. The purpose of partitioning is to
   A. manage complexity   B. ensure security
   C. use space efficiently   D. none of the above

   9._____

10. Blocking factor is used to represent   10.____
    A. storage of data in the adjacent memory locations
    B. per page physical records
    C. grouped attributes
    D. blocks of data

11. Which of the following is the best description of a secondary key?   11.____
    A. A key that represents a table
    B. Primary key
    C. A key alternate to the primary key
    D. A key that can hold duplicate values

12. Which of the following is used to describe the multi-dimensional databases? 12.____
    A. Relational database   B. Hierarchical database
    C. Data warehouse   D. Network model

13. Client server architecture does not reflect the following: 13.____
    A. It is necessary to have a file server
    B. Needs someone to forward the request
    C. Needs someone to respond to the forwarded request
    D. All of the above

14. Stored procedures have the advantage of   14.____
    A. efficiency with respect to data integrity, as different applications can have access to the same stored procedure
    B. faster traffic communication
    C. easier to write
    D. specially designed for client server mode

15. Which of the following is important for data warehouse architecture? 15.____
    A. Data mart
    B. Data may come from a number of sources that may either be internal or external
    C. Data is historical
    D. All of the above

16. A transactional system means which of the following? 16.____
    A. This is a system that is used for the purpose of carrying out daily transactions based on the live data
    B. This is a system used for the purpose of decision making based on live data
    C. This is a system that is used for decision making based on historical data
    D. This is a system that is used to carry out daily transactions based on historical data

17. All of the following are correct for a data warehouse EXCEPT
    A. it is utilized by the end users
    B. it is organized with respect to different subject areas
    C. historical data is held
    D. it is used for the purpose of decision making

17.____

18. What are fact tables?
    A. De-normalized structure in the data warehouse
    B. Data structure is partially normalized
    C. Completely normalized structure
    D. None of the above

18.____

19. What type of relationship exists in the dimension and fact table in the star schema?
    A. One to one   B. One to many
    C. Many to many   D. None of the above

19.____

20. A transactional manager is responsible for
    A. the maintenance of transactional logs
    B. holding and keeping track of the database images
    C. maintenance of concurrency control
    D. all of the above

20.____

21. A distributed system has the characteristic of
    A. cost efficiency   B. system complexity
    C. modular expansion   D. faster response

21.____

22. Em Friends();
    In the above statement, what represents the name of the class?
    A. Friends   B. Em
    C. Friends()   D. None of the above

23. Object definition language is used as a
    A. language for the object-oriented databases
    B. structured query language
    C. language to interpret the objects of an application
    D. all of the above

23.____

24. The advantage of ODBMS is
    A. it handles complex data on web
    B. it serves as an alternate of RDBMS for all types of applications
    C. its usability for the storage of historical data
    D. all of the above

24.____

25. The object query language has the structure that is much like SQL utilizing the structure of
    A. select-where   B. select-from-where
    C. where-select   D. none of the above

25.____

85

KEY (CORRECT ANSWERS)

1.	B		11.	C
2.	A		12.	C
3.	B		13.	A
4.	C		14.	A
5.	B		15.	D
6.	A		16.	A
7.	B		17.	A
8.	B		18.	C
9.	B		19.	B
10.	B		20.	D

21.	C
22.	B
23.	A
24.	A
25.	B

TEST 2

DIRECTIONS: Each question or incomplete statement is followed by several suggested answers or completions. Select the one that BEST answers the question or completes the statement. *PRINT THE LETTER OF THE CORRECT ANSWER IN THE SPACE AT THE RIGHT.*

1. What are the basic operations of a record management system?
   A. Adding records
   B. Updating records
   C. Deleting records
   D. All of the above

   1._____

2. A database management system is intended for
   A. program dependent data
   B. increase in data redundancy
   C. being accessible at many different places at a time
   D. all of the above

   2._____

3. Data dictionary is composed of
   A. database fields
   B. data types of database fields
   C. range and scope of database fields
   D. all of the above

   3._____

4. What is relational algebra?
   A. A language that defines data
   B. A meta definition language
   C. A procedural query language
   D. None of the above

   4._____

5. How is a weak entity represented in an E-R model?
   A. Diamond shape
   B. Solid rectangle
   C. Double outlined rectangle
   D. Circle

   5._____

6. Which of the following is FALSE about views?
   A. Results of views are based on the data of other tables
   B. View is considered as a virtual table
   C. Definition of view is part of the database
   D. Views are written in the form of a query

   6._____

7. With the use of data types,
   A. proper usage of data storage is performed
   B. data cannot be stored in non-relevant data types
   C. data integrity is enhanced
   D. all of the above

   7._____

8. If an entity does not contain an attribute which can uniquely determine the whole relation, then this entity is called _____ entity.
   A. child
   B. strong
   C. loose
   D. weak

   8._____

9. A join in which a table has a join with itself is termed as _____ join.   9._____
    A. self   B. inner
    C. outer   D. none of the above

10. What is logical schema?   10._____
    A. A database
    B. Information organization mechanism
    C. Data storage mechanism
    D. None of the above

11. Database anomalies are removed with the help of   11._____
    A. integrity constraints   B. normal forms
    C. dependencies   D. locking

12. Which of the following is the purpose of a trigger?   12._____
    A. Used to initiate different types of functions of DBMS
    B. A program statement used for the debugging purpose
    C. A function that validates a user
    D. A program code that is automatically run on the basis of some action on
       the database

13. Who is responsible for database supervision?   13._____
    A. Database administrator   B. Database manager
    C. DP manager   D. None of the above

14. Which of the following is TRUE about distributed database systems?   14._____
    A. Centralized and accessible at different locations
    B. Replication either partially or completely
    C. Segmentation at different places
    D. All of the above

15. Periodical change of data is termed as   15._____
    A. data update   B. data upgrade
    C. restructuring   D. none of the above

16. You can change the values of records using the command   16._____
    A. change   B. modify
    C. update   D. none of the above

17. The SQL comparison operators include   17._____
    A. =   B. >
    C. LIKE   D. all of the above

18. For two tables T1 and T2, the union operation will result in the retrieval of   18._____
    A. all rows of T1
    B. all rows of T2
    C. all rows of T1 and T2
    D. rows where all the rows in the two tables which have common columns

19. The word *enum* is used for which of the following?
    A. It establishes the range of values of an attribute
    B. It defines class range
    C. It represents a numeric value
    D. None of the above

19.____

20. _____ associations is a type of association supported with ODL.
    A. Unary   B. Binary
    C. Ternary   D. Unary and binary

20.____

21. Which of the following describes load and index in the BEST way?
    A. This process enhances the quality of data after it is moved to the data warehouse
    B. This is a process that creates data warehouse data and any required indexes are created
    C. This process enhances the quality of data before it is moved to the data warehouse
    D. This process rejects the inappropriate data from the data warehouse

21.____

22. Which of the following is TRUE with respect to two level data warehouse architecture?
    A. At minimum, one data mart is required
    B. Data coming from internal and external sources
    C. Real time updatable data
    D. None of the above

22.____

23. An index file master list
    A. is a sorted file
    B. is based on a list of keys and records
    C. contains each record with a specific number
    D. all of the above

23.____

24. If different columns of a table are located in different places, then it is called
    A. vertical portioning   B. replication
    C. horizontal portioning   D. none of the above

24.____

25. If we store different copies of a database at different locations, then it is called
    A. vertical portioning   B. replication
    C. horizontal portioning   D. none of the above

25.____

KEY (CORRECT ANSWERS)

1.	D		11.	A
2.	C		12.	D
3.	D		13.	A
4.	C		14.	D
5.	C		15.	A
6.	C		16.	C
7.	C		17.	D
8.	D		18.	D
9.	A		19.	A
10.	B		20.	D

21.	B
22.	B
23.	C
24.	A
25.	B

TEST 3

DIRECTIONS: Each question or incomplete statement is followed by several suggested answers or completions. Select the one that BEST answers the question or completes the statement. *PRINT THE LETTER OF THE CORRECT ANSWER IN THE SPACE AT THE RIGHT.*

1. Which of the following is the motive behind the development of database systems?
   A. More information reporting needs
   B. More information management needs
   C. Faster processing of real-time transactions
   D. All of the above

   1.____

2. Which of the following is the term used to refer to a set of data values?
   A. Attribute   B. Domain   C. Row   D. Degree

   2.____

3. The approach used to physically sort the records in a specific order is called
   A. hashing   B. sequential
   C. direct   D. none of the above

   3.____

4. What does cardinality mean?
   A. Number of tuples   B. Attributes count in a table
   C. Number of tables in the database   D. None of the above

   4.____

5. Which of the following refers to the cardinality?
   A. Properties   B. Degree   C. Relations   D. Cartesian

   5.____

6. If each cell of a relation contains an atomic value, then the relation scheme is in the _____ normal form.
   A. complete   B. first
   C. second   D. none of the above

   6.____

7. Sequence is saved in the
   A. database   B. relation
   C. data dictionary   D. database logs

   7.____

8. Which of the following symbols is used to represent attributes in an ER model?
   A. Ellipse   B. Rectangle
   C. Triangle   D. None of the above

   8.____

9. What type of key is used to reflect the relationship among different tables?
   A. Primary   B. Foreign   C. Secondary   D. Hash

   9.____

10. Extraction of some specific records from the database is termed
    A. join   B. selection   C. projection   D. grouping

    10.____

11. Benefits of sequential retrieval against primary key include   11._____
    A. fast processing   B. somewhat faster processing
    C. less resource utilization   D. none of the above

12. Changes of any type are visible from the cursor type of   12._____
    A. forward only   B. dynamic   C. keyset   D. static

13. The data in the DBMS is requested with the help of   13._____
    A. DDL   B. DML   C. VDL   D. SDL

14. The language which has become a standard for database interaction is   14._____
    A. DBASE   B. OQL   C. Oracle   D. SQL

15. What does SQL Count function do?   15._____
    A. Counts values   B. Counts distinct values
    C. Groups values   D. None of the above

16. DBMS helps achieve   16._____
    A. the independence of data
    B. a centralized control over the data
    C. data consistency
    D. all of the above

17. If you need to select on certain columns in your select query, which approach   17._____
will be used?
    A. Selection   B. Projection   C. Outer Join   D. Union

18. Which of the following commands is used for the deletion of a column in a   18._____
table?
    A. Alter   B. Update   C. Drop   D. Delete

19. Which of the following is TRUE concerning the following statement: 19._____
class Cat extends Animal?
    A. Cat is an abstract super class   B. Cat is an abstract sub class
    C. Cat is a concrete sub class   D. Cat is a concrete super class

20. Which of the following can be defined with ODL?   20._____
    A. Properties   B. Structure
    C. Functions   D. All of the above

21. What is the extract process?   21._____
    A. All the data from different operational systems is captured by this process
    B. This process captures a specific portion of data from different operational
       systems
    C. Data available with different decision support systems is captured by this
       process
    D. It captures specific data from a data warehouse

22. What is data transformation?
    A. This is a process that transforms the detailed level data into summary data
    B. Summary data is transformed into detailed data
    C. Data from one source is separated into different categories
    D. Data coming from different sources is combined at one place

22.____

23. What is data scrubbing?
    A. A mechanism that changes data into its appropriate form before moving to a data warehouse
    B. A mechanism that rejects the data out of a data warehouse
    C. This is a mechanism that enhances the quality of data warehouse data
    D. A data loading process

23.____

24. Which of the following is TRUE about lock files?
    A. Only one user can access the file
    B. Authenticated users can modify the file
    C. Its purpose is to secure the critical information
    D. All of the above

24.____

25. What is distributed database?
    A. One logical database that is distributed to multiple places
    B. A set of files distributed at different locations
    C. A database that is placed in one location in the logical form
    D. Database data distributed in different files at one place

25.____

KEY (CORRECT ANSWERS)

1.	D
2.	B
3.	A
4.	A
5.	D

6.	B
7.	C
8.	A
9.	B
10.	B

11.	A
12.	B
13.	B
14.	D
15.	A

16.	D
17.	B
18.	A
19.	C
20.	D

21.	B
22.	A
23.	A
24.	A
25.	A

TEST 4

DIRECTIONS: Each question or incomplete statement is followed by several suggested answers or completions. Select the one that BEST answers the question or completes the statement. *PRINT THE LETTER OF THE CORRECT ANSWER IN THE SPACE AT THE RIGHT.*

1. A DBMS may carry on information processing with _____ systems.   1._____
   A. word processing   B. spreadsheet processing
   C. graphical   D. all of the above

2. A combination of which of the following makes up a database record?   2._____
   A. Attributes   B. Tuples
   C. Entities   D. None of the above

3. Strong keys refer to the entities having _____ keys.   3._____
   A. primary   B. candidate
   C. unique   D. none of the above

4. The purpose of report generator is to _____ data.   4._____
   A. update   B. add   C. delete   D. view and print

5. What is conceptual design?   5._____
   A. Used for the purpose of documentation
   B. Graphical view of the database
   C. Database modeling irrespective of DBMS
   D. Relational model design

6. Which of the following determines the physical location of a record?   6._____
   A. Binary tree   B. Sequence
   C. Hashing   D. Indexing

7. In which model are records organized in the form of a tree?   7._____
   A. Network   B. Hierarchical   C. Network   D. Relational

8. Which type of dependency is NOT allowed in the second normal form?   8._____
   A. Full   B. Loose
   C. Partial   D. None of the above

9. Fifth normal form refers to   9._____
   A. data atomicity   B. fully functional dependency
   C. join dependency   D. none of the above

10. Entity integrity with respect to primary keys infers that it must be   10._____
    A. not null   B. unique
    C. both A and B   D. none of the above

11. During the DBMS operations, which of the following are used?
    A. Data dictionary   B. Transaction log
    C. Both A and B   D. None of the above

11.____

12. Entities properties are also termed as
    A. relations   B. rows
    C. attributes   D. none of the above

12.____

13. How is natural join performed?
    A. It is based on Cartesian product
    B. Union and Cartesian products are both performed
    C. Projection and Cartesian products are both performed
    D. None of the above

13.____

14. Which type of lock can enforce an item to be read but not modified?
    A. Shared   B. Exclusive   C. Explicit   D. Implicit

14.____

15. For a relation,
    A. data can be stored in any sequence
    B. there is no duplication of data
    C. both A and B are true
    D. none of the above

15.____

16. What is NULL?
    A. Equivalent to 0
    B. Equivalent to space
    C. 0 for numeric value and space for character value
    D. No value

16.____

17. The relationship among two entities is referred to as
    A. unary   B. quaternary   C. ternary   D. binary

17.____

18. If there are two relations named R1 and R2 with x number of tuples for R1 and y tuples for R2, then the maximum number of join results is
    A. $(x+y)/2$ B. $(x+y)*2$ C. $x+y$ D. xy

18.____

19. Committed changes become permanent with the transaction of
    A. atomic   B. durable
    C. consistent   D. none of the above

19.____

20. Which of the following functions may be performed with ODL?
    A. A complete data set including the duplicates may be returned
    B. A complete data set without the duplicates may be returned
    C. A specific data subset may be returned
    D. All of the above

20.____

21. Which of the following is an atomic literal?
    A. Boolean   B. Strings
    C. Character   D. All of the above

21.____

22. What is transient data?
    A. Data that is not available in case any changes to the existing data is made
    B. Data that is not eliminated in case any changes to the data are made
    C. Unchangeable data
    D. Permanent undeletable data

22.____

23. Which of the following is reconciled data?
    A. Transactional data of the organization
    B. One source of data to support all the decision-making processes
    C. Selected pieces of data
    D. None of the above

23.____

24. What is the objective of a data-mining process?
    A. Extract vital patterns and trends hidden in the data
    B. Composed of a set of algorithms that help find patterns of data
    C. It is best suited with historical data stored in the data warehouse
    D. All of the above

24.____

25. Which of the following is TRUE about replication?
    A. Network traffic is reduced
    B. On the failure of database at one site, the database at the other site may be utilized
    C. Storage capacity at each site must be the same
    D. None of the above

25.____

KEY (CORRECT ANSWERS)

1.	D		11.	C
2.	A		12.	C
3.	A		13.	C
4.	D		14.	A
5.	C		15.	C
6.	C		16.	D
7.	B		17.	D
8.	C		18.	D
9.	D		19.	B
10.	C		20.	D

21. D
22. A
23. B
24. D
25. C

EXAMINATION SECTION

TEST 1

DIRECTIONS: Each question or incomplete statement is followed by several suggested answers or completions. Select the one that BEST answers the question or completes the statement. *PRINT THE LETTER OF THE CORRECT ANSWER IN THE SPACE AT THE RIGHT.*

1. Which of the following languages could be used for the programming of a mobile application?

    A. C++   B. Java   C. PHP   D. A and B only

    1.____

2. Which version of the iOS supports multitasking?

    A. All versions   B. iOS4 and above
    C. iOS4   D. None

    2.____

3. In iOS, _____ control(s) the presentation of an app's content on the screen.

    A. UI controller   B. view controller objects
    C. UI objects   D. controller objects

    3.____

4. _____ are important considerations for mobile applications.

    A. Business case and platform   B. USP and SDK
    C. SDK and business case   D. Emulator and SDK

    4.____

5. A mobile application can access

    A. application specific data
    B. personal and device location data
    C. device location
    D. application specific data, personal and device location data

    5.____

6. AAPT is a packaging tool specifically used for

    A. Android   B. iOS
    C. Windows phone   D. both A and B

    6.____

7. Android architecture is composed of _____ key components.

    A. five   B. three   C. two   D. four

    7.____

8. ADB is associated only with

    A. iOS   B. Android
    C. both A and B   D. Windows

    8.____

9. Does the iPhone browser support Flash files?

    A. Yes   B. No
    C. Only those developed by Apple   D. Specific versions

    9.____

10. On Apple devices, Facetime is associated with
    A. digital photos   B. video calls
    C. editing photos   D. taking videos

10.____

11. If a mobile application is not working, what should be considered FIRST?
    A. Troubleshooting through application page
    B. Add notifications
    C. Both A and B
    D. Restart the device

11.____

12. X-code can be used only in
    A. iOS   B. OS X   C. Android   D. Both A and B

12.____

13. Setting permission is important in mobile application development because permission applies restrictions on
    A. data   B. code   C. both A and B   D. the device

13.____

14. On an Apple device, while registering the app, sometimes the configuration profile fails to install because
    A. there is no Internet access
    B. the app cannot connect to the HCP
    C. the app version on the mobile device is not supported by the application server
    D. the user is trying to register with a different HCP

14.____

15. Some of the well-known issues associated with iOS include
    A. Quick type, Facetime and save messages
    B. Facetime and hanging of applications
    C. Save messages and video sharing
    D. Quick type and sending files

15.____

16. If the file viewer is experiencing an error, what is a possible solution?
    A. Turn off the device
    B. Initiate Airplane Mode
    C. Turn off>turn on>view file again
    D. Turn on Wi-Fi

16.____

17. Which of the following is a likely reason that a mobile app cannot connect to the HCP system?
    A. No Internet access   B. SSL server certificate
    C. Both A and B   D. Application is expired

17.____

18. Which of the following JSON framework is supported by IOS?
    A. SBJson   B. Ajax
    C. Json-rpc   D. Both A and C

18.____

19. Which of the following frameworks is used to construct application user's interface for iOS?
    A. UIKit framework
    B. SDK
    C. IOS SDK
    D. Both A and C

19.____

20. What are the tools required to develop iOS applications?
    A. Intel-based Macintosh computer
    B. iOS SDK
    C. Both A and B
    D. SDK

20.____

21. In iOS, UIWindow object is responsible for the presentation of
    A. single view
    B. multiple views
    C. screen
    D. icon only

21.____

22. Android displays a status for non-responsive applications which is named as
    A. ANR
    B. NRA
    C. RAN
    D. both A and B

22.____

23. Android debug bridge specifically controls
    A. intent filters
    B. icons and labels
    C. permissions
    D. communication concerning emulator port

23.____

24. In Android application development, intent is used to start a new
    A. activity
    B. class
    C. instance
    D. both A and B

24.____

25. Which one of the following is the MOST popular language for Android applications?
    A. Java
    B. Asp.Net
    C. PHP
    D. Object pascal

25.____

KEY (CORRECT ANSWERS)

1.	D		11.	C
2.	D		12.	D
3.	B		13.	C
4.	A		14.	A
5.	D		15.	A
6.	A		16.	C
7.	D		17.	C
8.	B		18.	A
9.	A		19.	A
10.	B		20.	C

21.	B
22.	A
23.	D
24.	A
25.	A

TEST 2

DIRECTIONS: Each question or incomplete statement is followed by several suggested answers or completions. Select the one that BEST answers the question or completes the statement. *PRINT THE LETTER OF THE CORRECT ANSWER IN THE SPACE AT THE RIGHT.*

1. In general, mobile application development life cycle consists of _____ phase(s).
    A. five B. four C. three D. one

    1._____

2. Xamarin offers single language C#, which could be used for
    A. Android, iOS, Windows phone
    B. iOS
    C. Windows phone and Symbian
    D. iOS and Windows phone

    2._____

3. Which of the following is included in Xamarin?
    A. Modern Language Constructs   B. Amazing Base Class Library
    C. Web services   D. Both A and B

    3._____

4. Which one of the following is the BEST choice to develop cross-platform mobile applications?
    A. Xamarin   B. Objective-C
    C. Swift and Java   D. PHP

    4._____

5. SQLite database engine is used for _____-based mobile applications.
    A. iOS   B. Android
    C. iOS and Android   D. Symbian

    5._____

6. The MOST basic function of Portable Class Library is to
    A. distribute assemblies   B. build assemblies
    C. create cross-platform solution D. both A and B

    6._____

7. Mobile applications which are built using Xamarin also use _____ web services.
    A. REST, SOUP and WCF   B. SOUP
    C. WCF and REST   D. all of the above

    7._____

8. Which of the following commercial services are used for notifications in mobile applications?
    A. Urban Airship   B. Windows Azure
    C. PushSharp   D. A and B only

    8._____

9. iOS and _____ provide means for interpreting patterns of touches into gestures.
    A. Android   B. Symbian   C. Windows   D. Blackberry

    9._____

10. Assets folder created for Android includes _____ files.   10._____
    A. Text, font, XML, audio and video   B. XML
    C. music and video   D. HTML

11. Android asset packaging tools deal with   11._____
    A. zip compatible archives   B. cross-platform applications
    C. storage   D. B and C only

12. In Android environment, which one of the following describes the purpose   12._____
of Emulator?
    A. Write code + test code
    B. Debug code + test code + write code
    C. Test code
    D. Write code

13. Store Kit APIs are used to sell digital products and services only in   13._____
    A. iOS   B. Android   C. Symbian   D. both A and B

14. Which one of the following is the MOST acceptable use of images in iOS   14._____
applications?
    A. Resolution independent images
    B. Asset catalog, image sets, images in code, resolution independent
       images
    C. Images in code
    D. Both A and C

15. On Android devices, when multiple files are sent to another app, some files   15._____
could not be downloaded. This is because
    A. the app cannot connect to the HCP
    B. one or more files have larger size than the limit
    C. HCP is not responding
    D. A and B only

16. When the file viewer is experiencing an error, what is the possible outcome?   16._____
    A. File content is blank   B. File sending is failed
    C. Both A and B   D. File becomes corrupt

17. If the storage quota has been exceeded, what are the possible solutions?   17._____
    A. Delete and remove files from synced folder
    B. Increase storage quota by asking administrator
    C. Both A and B
    D. Buy memory card

18. What is the purpose of containers in Android applications?   18._____
    A. Hold objects and widgets   B. ProgressDialog
    C. Assist in display   D. Notifications

19. Android application architecture is based on
    A. intent
    B. resource
    C. notification
    D. content providers

    19._____

20. Which one of the following is a storage method for Android?
    A. SQLite database
    B. MYSQL
    C. SQL2008
    D. Both A and B

    20._____

21. Android Open-source project is responsible to maintain
    A. new versions and compatibility
    B. Android software and cross-platform support
    C. compatibility
    D. Cross-platform support

    21._____

22. Which one of the following is related to the iOS?
    A. Multitasking, SBJson, UIKit framework
    B. SBJson
    C. UIKit framework
    D. Multitasking

    22._____

23. Which API in iOS is used to write test scripts that assist the running of an application's user interface elements?
    A. UI Automation API
    B. UI API
    C. Automation API
    D. Both A and B

    23._____

24. An application in iOS is an active application when it is
    A. receiving events
    B. running in foreground
    C. running in background
    D. both A and B

    24._____

25. In iOS, UIKit classes could be used by
    A. all threads
    B. application's main thread
    C. single thread
    D. both A and B

    25._____

KEY (CORRECT ANSWERS)

1.	A		11.	A
2.	A		12.	B
3.	D		13.	A
4.	A		14.	B
5.	C		15.	D
6.	D		16.	C
7.	A		17.	C
8.	D		18.	A
9.	A		19.	D
10.	A		20.	A

21.	A
22.	A
23.	A
24.	D
25.	B

EXAMINATION SECTION
TEST 1

DIRECTIONS: Each question or incomplete statement is followed by several suggested answers or completions. Select the one that BEST answers the question or completes the statement. *PRINT THE LETTER OF THE CORRECT ANSWER IN THE SPACE AT THE RIGHT.*

1. Which of the following is NOT a step of Information System Audit Process?   1._____
   A. Planning
   B. Studying/Testing and Evaluating Controls
   C. Interfacing
   D. Reporting

2. Controlled disclosure of information is known as   2._____
   A. privacy   B. security   C. integrity   D. confidentiality

3. The maintenance of fault tolerance, DR, backup and storage procedures falls under _____ Review.   3._____
   A. Network Security   B. Business Continuity
   C. Data Integrity   D. Environment

4. The document that contains the objectives, accountability and responsibility for the IS Audit is known as   4._____
   A. Audit Charter   B. Software Charter
   C. Audit Report   D. Audit Plan

5. Subject Matter Criteria should be   5._____
   A. subjective and objective   B. objective and accountable
   C. objective and measurable   D. complete and subjective

6. Which one of the following is NOT a step for Risk Management Process Area?   6._____
   A. Risk Ignorance   B. Risk Measurement
   C. Risk Monitoring   D. Risk Mitigation

7. Which is the correct sequence of IT Process Optimization steps?   7._____
   I.   Identify and prioritize business process
   II.   Finalize optimization techniques
   III. As-is process analysis
   IV.   Implementation
   V.   To-be process mapping

   The CORRECT answer is:
   A. I, II, III, IV, V   B. I, III, II, V, IV
   C. I, III, IV, II, V   D. I, II, IV, V, III

8.	_____ is accountable for the internal IT and Environmental Organizational controls.	8.____
- A. Audit Committee
- B. Management
- C. Auditor
- D. Lead Auditor

9.	COBIT Framework is referred to yield the organizational maturity in	9.____
- A. IT Governance
- B. IS Audit
- C. IS Security
- D. Audit Planning

10.	Reviewing the extent of Project Management Techniques applied in an organization is done under _____ Planning.	10.____
- A. Strategic
- B. Business Strategic
- C. Audit
- D. Tactical

11.	The document defining the justification of a project for its implementation is known as	11.____
- A. Project Plan
- B. Project Timeline
- C. Business Case
- D. Test Case

12.	Incidence Reports should be reviewed during _____ Review.	12.____
- A. BCP
- B. Governance
- C. Business Case
- D. Network Security

13.	Which is the missing testing phase among the following: Pretest; Post-test; Post-invocation?	13.____
- A. Preliminary Test
- B. Test
- C. Detailed Test
- D. Test Case

14.	Measuring that the risk analysis is performed routinely is done under which aspect of BCP?	14.____
- A. Organizational
- B. Departmental
- C. Planning
- D. Procedural

15.	Business Impact Analysis is performed before the implementation of	15.____
- A. Audit Planning
- B. Requirement Verification
- C. Business Continuity Plan
- D. Risk Assessment

16.	Which phase is missing in the following list of SDLC phases: Business requirements definition; Design and development (construction); Testing; Implementation; Post-implementation?	16.____
- A. Business Case
- B. Project Initiation
- C. Project Maintenance
- D. Project Support

17.	Requirement Sign-off is done under which phase?	17.____
- A. Project Initiation
- B. Implementation
- C. Post implementation
- D. Business requirements definition

18. A _____ is developed in order to maintain control of the project during its entire life cycle.
    A. Project Master Plan   B. Project Scope Document
    C. Project Milestone   D. Business Case

  18.____

19. Which of the following plans covers the Issue Logging and Tracking?
    A. Project Plan   B. Project Initiating Plan
    C. Risk Plan   D. QA Plan

  19.____

20. A feasibility study should involve the following: critical personnel, business personnel, QA personnel and
    A. management   B. executive staff
    C. technical staff   D. customers

  20.____

21. Identification of telecommunication access paths into and out of the organization's premises is known as
    A. tracking   B. rogue access jacks
    C. accessibility control   D. routing control

  21.____

22. Hard-coded MAC addresses lead to
    A. data loss   B. incident reporting
    C. wireless vulnerability   D. project issue

  22.____

23. Encryption login credentials are used to maintain
    A. integrity   B. accessibility
    C. confidentiality   D. privacy

  23.____

24. Assuring that data is not changed means
    A. integrity   B. confidentiality
    C. security   D. privacy

  24.____

25. A very essential requirement for electronic payment is
    A. encryption   B. nonrepudiation
    C. authentication   D. authorization

  25.____

KEY (CORRECT ANSWERS)

1.	C		11.	C
2.	D		12.	A
3.	B		13.	B
4.	A		14.	A
5.	C		15.	C
6.	A		16.	B
7.	B		17.	D
8.	B		18.	A
9.	A		19.	D
10.	D		20.	C

21.	B
22.	C
23.	C
24.	A
25.	B

TEST 2

1. Which of the following is NOT the main area for IS Audit?
   A. Availability
   B. Integrity
   C. Controllability
   D. Confidentiality

   1._____

2. Which of the following provides a high level of assurance regarding the effectiveness of control procedures?
   A. Review
   B. Audit
   C. Peer Review
   D. Test

   2._____

3. The internal audit plan must be approved by the
   A. auditor
   B. audit committee
   C. audit charter
   D. reviewer

   3._____

4. Which of the following does NOT fall under the scope of the audit?
   A. People
   B. Date
   C. Application systems
   D. Inventory

   4._____

5. _____ is known as the defined information in the auditor report and the procedures defining the controls operation and its compliance with IS Auditing Standards.
   A. Subject matter
   B. Subject report
   C. Subject criteria
   D. Audit charter

   5._____

6. The process to check whether the Organization Mission and objective is aligned with the IS function is covered in
   A. Risk Assessment
   B. IT Governance
   C. Organizational Maturity Models
   D. Planning Guidelines

   6._____

7. Application controls are defined as the grouped controls within
   A. application   B. software   C. hardware   D. organization

   7._____

8. Data analysis techniques help to monitor the _____ of the system.
   A. robustness
   B. scalability
   C. extendibility
   D. reliability

   8._____

9. The issues highlighted related to IT Governance must escalate to
   A. management
   B. higher management
   C. stakeholders/people
   D. auditors

   9._____

10. The strategy to follow the measures that reduce the likelihood for a risk to occur is known as risk
    A. identification
    B. measurement
    C. management
    D. mitigation

10.____

11. Two parameters for risk management are
    A. likelihood and severity
    B. consequences and measures
    C. mitigation and likelihood
    D. severity and follow-up

11.____

12. Which one of the following is NOT a fundamental aspect of Benefits Realization Approach?
    A. Project Management
    B. Portfolio Management
    C. Service Catalog Management
    D. Full Cycle Governance

12.____

13. Which of the following is NOT a BCP Aspect of Review?
    A. Organizational
    B. Departmental
    C. Planning
    D. Procedural

13.____

14. What identifies the crucial recovery time frames of the critical business processes?
    A. Business impact analysis
    B. Business continuity
    C. Business case
    D. Business realization approaches

14.____

15. Planning of the periodic review of risk is done under which aspect of BCP?
    A. Organizational
    B. Planning
    C. Procedural
    D. Monitoring

15.____

16. When defining the system alternative solutions, which of the following should be given LEAST priority?
    A. System enhancements
    B. Manual solutions
    C. Vendor solutions
    D. In-house design and development

16.____

17. Verification of vendor agreements is done at
    A. business requirements definition
    B. design and development (construction)
    C. testing
    D. implementation

17.____

18. Legal and security requirements are identified during
    A. process audit
    B. requirement definition
    C. implementation
    D. support

18.____

19. A test plan should define which of the following roles for a test result?
    A. Reviewing and approver
    B. Author and reviewer
    C. Reviewer and manager
    D. Approver and author

19.____

20. _____ review should be done to make sure that the project has met user expectations, project and timeline.   20.____
    A. QA   B. Network
    C. Development   D. Implementation

21. A system which validates that the public key belongs to the individual or organization is called the _____ system.   21.____
    A. KPI   B. PKI   C. SDLC   D. testing

22. _____ is the way of authenticating the sending of a message.   22.____
    A. PKI   B. Encryption
    C. Cryptography   D. Digital signature

23. PKI stands for   23.____
    A. Public Key Infrastructure   B. Private Key Infrastructure
    C. Public Key Identifier   D. Private Key Identifier

24. Secure Sockets Layer/Transport Layer Security (SSL/TLS) is used for encryption of   24.____
    A. HTTP   B. TCP   C. UDP   D. TTIP

25. The _____ digitally signs the certificate in order to validate that the public key belongs to the authorized owner.   25.____
    A. PKI   B. KPI   C. CA   D. SSL

KEY (CORRECT ANSWERS)

1.	C		11.	A
2.	B		12.	C
3.	B		13.	B
4.	D		14.	A
5.	A		15.	B
6.	B		16.	B
7.	A		17.	A
8.	D		18.	B
9.	B		19.	A
10.	D		20.	D

21.	B
22.	D
23.	A
24.	A
25.	C

EXAMINATION SECTION

TEST 1

DIRECTIONS: Each question or incomplete statement is followed by several suggested answers or completions. Select the one that BEST answers the question or completes the statement. *PRINT THE LETTER OF THE CORRECT ANSWER IN THE SPACE AT THE RIGHT.*

1. Assume you are the security officer of an organization. The major duties involved are to record security-related information, as well as writing a manual that can be referred to by the company's other employees in case you are absent. Specify which of the following documents need to be added to your manual that would be used to perform a specific task. 1.____
   A. Procedures   B. Guidelines   C. Policies   D. Business case

2. Assume you are the administrator of a bank. A user calls to tell you he has been notified to contact the bank personnel but he is not able to find the contact details on the company website. A few days ago, the user had actually received an e-mail stating that there had been some issue with his bank account and that he needed to click a specific link. The user clicked on the link and gave his personal details. After this incident, his account is now showing large numbers of transactions not done by the user himself. The user has turned out to be the victim of 2.____
   A. DDoS
   C. man-in-the-middle
   B. DoS
   D. phishing

3. You are working in an organization as a junior administrator. You are going through the log files and found that an intruder has been trying to make use of an IP address in order to substitute some other system in the network to get access. This type of attack is known as 3.____
   A. TCP/IP Hijacking
   C. DoS
   B. virus
   D. backdoor

4. You are working as a security administrator. While going through the network health, you find out that a threat is making rounds. The last attack tried to intervene in a communication by adding up a system within the communicating entities. This type of attack is known as 4.____
   A. backdoor
   C. man-in-the-middle
   B. virus
   D. worm

5. While working over your system, the keyboard gets hanged. After making several tries, you notice that it only occurs when you open a specific spreadsheet, as well as connected to the internet. This type of attack is known as 5.____
   A. man-in-the-middle
   C. logic bomb
   B. worm
   D. phage virus

6. You are working as the network security administrator in a company. You are
receiving complaints from a lot of users regarding the system being infected by
antivirus software. The system infection pop-up message is the same for every
user. The BEST suited situation of the following is:
A. It is a DoS attack
B. A worm virus is infecting each and every system
C. The anti-virus is outdated
D. The server is acting as a virus carrier

6.____

7. While going through the log files of the network, you come to know that there
is a continuous attempt in order to access one particular account. The MOST
appropriate type of attack is
A. password guessing   B. phage virus
C. backdoor   D. worm

7.____

8. While working on your computer, you notice that your hard disk is working
very actively when you are not performing any activity over it. The system is
also not connected to the internet. The MOST appropriate type of situation
your system is going through is
A. hard disk failure
B. DoS attack
C. virus is replicating in the system
D. worm

8.____

9. While working as an administrator of a company, one of your tasks is to
monitor the monthly reports and logs to check for any discrepancies. For the
past month, when viewing the e-mail error log report, you find that there had
been many attempts to log on. The type of attack targeting the e-mail server is
A. worm   B. virus
C. backdoor   D. software exploitation

9.____

10. You have downloaded a file from the internet. Since then you have noticed
a strange behavior in your system. You check that the virus definition file is
missing from the system. The MOST appropriate type of system infection is
A. retrovirus   B. phage virus   C. backdoor   D. worm

10.____

11. The kind of attack where the attacker logs in as a normal user and then
enhances the rights assigned to that particular user in order to perform further
actions is known as
A. footprinting   B. privilege breach
C. privilege escalation   D. privilege attack

11.____

12. When a dumpster diver is looking through an organization's trash bin, which
of the following is the LEAST important?
A. IP address list   B. E-mail addresses
C. Network diagram   D. Public website page proof

12.____

13. Which of the following is the method used to prevent the user from the installation of any software that is not approved by the client?
    A. Privilege restriction
    B. Signing the acceptable use policy
    C. Audit report
    D. Anti-virus

13.____

14. Which of the following is considered a PKI security breach?
    A. Knowing the public key
    B. Getting the encrypted message
    C. Information regarding the type of encryption used
    D. Private key disclosure

14.____

15. User A wants to send an encrypted message to User B. For this purpose, two things are required: a session key and a(n)
    A. User B public key   B. User B private key
    C. KPI   D. hash algorithm

15.____

16. The type of situation in which the computer chips are not working properly due to cyclical temperature fluctuations is known as
    A. crosstalk   B. switching   C. chip creep   D. routing

16.____

17. When you are provided with a new patch for the server OS, what step needs to be performed?
    A. Roll out patch without testing
    B. Avoid all non-mission-critical patches
    C. Make a plan for patch installation
    D. Test the patch within a controlled environment

17.____

18. The type of process that can prevent the e-mail server from sending the fake source e-mail address messages is known as
    A. DNS reverse lookup   B. authorized list
    C. encryption   D. authorization checks

18.____

19. Which one of the following is NOT the active response taken by the IDS in case of intrusion detection?
    A. Changing environment
    B. Sending information to the administrator
    C. Disconnecting session
    D. Allowing additional auditing parameters

19.____

20. A particular subnet within a network consists of four servers that frequently transfer large amounts of data. These servers do not need to interact with any other type of device in the network, although the devices which are in the subnet do need to communicate with the rest of the network. Which of the following tools is the BEST to manage the interaction among subnet and the rest of the network?
    A. Proxy server   B. Tunnel   C. Router   D. Switch

20.____

21. Which of the following is the basic problem that reduces firewall effectiveness?
    A. Large amount of traffic
    B. High speed traffic
    C. Encrypted traffic
    D. Low traffic

21.____

22. Which of the following is referred to as the standard for governing encryption?
    A. PKI
    B. PKCS
    C. ISA
    D. SSL

22.____

23. Which of the following components is used in order to collect IDS data?
    A. Sensor
    B. Event
    C. Analyzer
    D. Source

23.____

24. Which of the following mechanisms are employed by the PKI in order to perform immediate verification concerning certificate validity?
    A. SSHA
    B. SSHA-1
    C. SSHA-11
    D. OCSP

24.____

25. Which of the following types of systems can be used to offer active protection as well as identification/notification of security issues within that network connected to the internet?
    A. Router
    B. IDS
    C. Switch
    D. Network monitoring

25.____

KEY (CORRECT ANSWERS)

1.	B		11.	C
2.	D		12.	D
3.	A		13.	B
4.	C		14.	D
5.	C		15.	A
6.	D		16.	C
7.	A		17.	D
8.	C		18.	A
9.	D		19.	B
10.	A		20.	C

21.	C
22.	B
23.	A
24.	D
25.	B

TEST 2

DIRECTIONS: Each question or incomplete statement is followed by several suggested answers or completions. Select the one that BEST answers the question or completes the statement. *PRINT THE LETTER OF THE CORRECT ANSWER IN THE SPACE AT THE RIGHT.*

1. The supervisor of the company you are working for is busy and requests you to login the HR server by making use of his login credentials and render some of the required reports. What possible action should be taken by you?
   A. Do as the supervisor requested.
   B. Ignore the supervisor's request.
   C. Don't follow the request and explain to the supervisor that it is against the policy.
   D. Complain to the higher management.

   1.____

2. You are working as the development team lead in a company. You receive the following e-mail from the helpdesk:
   Dear Organization Users:
   From the next week, all inactive e-mail accounts will be deleted to spare more space for new users. For this particular reason, you are required to send us your e-mail details so that your e-mail addresses may continue to work.
   The required information is:
   - Name
   - E-mail
   - Password
   - DOB

   Which of the following is this type of attack?
   A. Man-in-the-middle   B. DoS
   C. DDoS   D. Phishing

   2.____

3. Some of your friends have sent you an electronic greeting over your official e-mail address. To be able to view the card you need to click on an attachment. Which of the following possible steps should you take at this particular point?
   A. Open the attachment
   B. Leave the message
   C. Delete the message
   D. Forward the card to other employees in the organization

   3.____

4. Which of the following meets the UCSC's password requirements?
   A. @#$)*###   B. akRGkmutM   C. UcSc4Evr!   D. Password123

   4.____

5. While working on the system, you notice that the mouse over the computer screen has started to move by itself and starts clicking over items on the desktop. Which possible action should you take?
   - A. Call someone for help
   - B. Disconnect the computer from the network
   - C. Call helpdesk
   - D. Run anti-virus

   5.____

6. You are working as the security administrator. A user has called you to report that he downloaded a file from a client through IM. Since the file was downloaded, the system behavior is unusual. What has occurred?
   - A. Your user downloaded a virus using IM
   - B. The user has a defective hard drive
   - C. Power issues
   - D. User is hallucinating

   6.____

7. While working as the network administrator, you find out that you have limited resources and you wish to keep the network as secure as possible. Which of the following measures will you take?
   - A. Use hash algorithm
   - B. Reduce the logging levels of the network audit files
   - C. Use symmetric algorithm
   - D. IDS

   7.____

8. In your company, the security manager has asked you to implement port mirroring. Which particular mechanism will you apply in order to implement port spanning or mirroring?
   - A. Cisco's Switched Port Analyzer (SPAN)
   - B. SSHA
   - C. SSHA-1
   - D. RADIUS

   8.____

9. The security manager from your organization asked you to remove all the unused software, services as well as processed from the workstations. The reason for this is that these unused software can be used to cause exploitation. The process you are following by agreeing to the security manager is
   - A. protocol analyzing
   - B. spamming
   - C. IDS implementation
   - D. platform hardening

   9.____

10. Suppose you wish to connect to a remote system which has an IP address 192.168.0.100, which is running a website. Port 80 would be used by default. The socket description in this case will be
    - A. 192.168.0.100:80.80
    - B. 80.192.168.0.100
    - C. 80:192.168.0.100:80
    - D. 192.168.0.100:80

    10.____

11. Which of the following mechanisms is utilized in order to investigate the system to find out the clues of an event?
    - A. Anti-virus scanning
    - B. Application of security policies
    - C. KPI
    - D. Computer forensics

    11.____

12. Which of the following mechanisms are utilized for the individual role in the organization?

    A. DAC   B. SSHA   C. RBAC   D. STAC

12.____

13. You wish to give access to the network by using the retina scan authentication method. Which one of the following methods makes use of a physical characteristic for authenticating identity?

    A. Biometric   B. Smart Card
    C. Identity Card   D. IDS

13.____

14. Which of the following options has the fastest backup method?

    A. Full backup   B. Incremental backup
    C. Derivative backup   D. Archival backup

14.____

15. An organization has hired you as the security consultant. The organization is interested in the implementation of handheld devices, for example PDA's. For this, the company policy is to make use of the asymmetric system. Which of the following security standards will you recommend in this case?

    A. ECC   B. PKI   C. SHA   D. MD

15.____

16. Which of the following algorithms should be used for the creation of the temporary secure session concerning key info exchange?

    A. KEA   B. Hashing algorithm
    C. SSL   D. SSHA

16.____

17. An organization has a lot of policies regarding security issues. Which of the following policies is actually used that describes the computer usage in the organization?

    A. Security policy   B. User policy
    C. Use policy   D. Enforcement policy

17.____

18. _____ is defined as the encryption method utilizing one message to hide another.

    A. Steganography   B. Hashing
    C. SSL   D. Crypto-analysis

18.____

19. Which of the following is the BEST option that can offer extra security over the web server?

    A. Changing the port address to 8080
    B. Changing the port address to 1019
    C. Adding a firewall to block port 80
    D. Application of encryption techniques

19.____

20. Which of the following is the equivalent option to a VLAN w.r.t. physical security perspective?

    A. Perimeter security   B. Partitioning
    C. Encryption   D. IDS

20.____

21. The goal of integrity deals with the verification that
    A. data is kept private
    B. information is accurate
    C. security constraints are implemented
    D. access control techniques are implemented

21.____

22. Which of the following protocols is utilized to establish a secure session in a wireless network?
    A. WAP   B. WEP   C. WTLS   D. WML

22.____

23. When dealing with the DOD model, the internet server interfaces with TCP/IP at which layer?
    A. Transport   B. Network   C. Process   D. Internet

23.____

24. In order to create a network connection among the two LAN's using internet, what technology should be implied?
    A. IPSec   B. L2TP   C. PPP   D. SLIP

24.____

25. Which of the following methods can be used in order to enable/disable network access on the basis of IP address?
    A. Partitioning   B. Hardening
    C. Steganography   D. ACL

25.____

KEY (CORRECT ANSWERS)

1.	C		11.	D
2.	D		12.	C
3.	C		13.	A
4.	C		14.	B
5.	B		15.	A
6.	A		16.	A
7.	B		17.	C
8.	A		18.	A
9.	D		19.	B
10.	D		20.	B

21.	B
22.	B
23.	C
24.	B
25.	D

TEST 3

DIRECTIONS: Each question or incomplete statement is followed by several suggested answers or completions. Select the one that BEST answers the question or completes the statement. *PRINT THE LETTER OF THE CORRECT ANSWER IN THE SPACE AT THE RIGHT.*

1. Authentication is defined as the basic content used for
   A. control   B. policies   C. security   D. Performance

   1.____

2. The term *intruder* is defined as the security threat referring to
   A. data loss   B. data access
   C. data modification   D. hacker or cracker

   2.____

3. The very fundamental security issue faced in designing OS is to
   A. control   B. apply corrective action
   C. remove   D. prevent

   3.____

4. Access control tends to implement the _____ policy.
   A. control   B. user   C. security   D. access

   4.____

5. Sensors are used for data
   A. removal   B. deletion   C. collection   D. manipulation

   5.____

6. Which of the following tends to be defined as the basic security threat?
   A. File deletion   B. File shredding
   C. File encryption   D. File sharing

   6.____

7. Which of the following is NOT file permission?
   A. Stop   B. Write   C. Execute   D. Read

   7.____

8. While assigning permissions, which one of the following is a GOOD approach?
   A. Grant full permission
   B. Grant read-only permission
   C. Grant limited permission to a particular user
   D. Grant read and write but not the execute permission

   8.____

9. Which of the following is the LEAST secure means of authentication?
   A. Keycard   B. Eye retina detection
   C. Fingerprint   D. Password

   9.____

10. A one-time password is considered to be safe because it
    A. generates easily   B. won't be shared
    C. is different with every access   D. is an encrypted one

    10.____

11. Which of these two processes occur first, *authentication* or *authorization*?
    A. Authentication   B. Authorization
    C. Parallel   D. Both are the same

    11.____

12. The type of attack that tends to make a system or resource NOT available to the resources is known as
    A. DoS
    B. man-in-the-middle
    C. phishing
    D. worm

12._____

13. The particular code part which is intended to misuse the environment is known as
    A. code stacker
    B. Trojan horse
    C. network thief
    D. code exploiter

13._____

14. Which of the following patterns is used in order to determine a virus?
    A. Stealth
    B. Phage
    C. Digital Signature
    D. Virus Signature

14._____

15. Which of the following attacks makes use of a spawn process to effect system efficiency?
    A. Worm
    B. Virus
    C. Trojan
    D. DoS

15._____

16. The MOST appropriate match with asymmetric encryption is:
    A. Same key is generated for encryption and decryption
    B. Different keys are generated for encryption and decryption
    C. There is no concept of keys
    D. All keys are shared with all users

16._____

17. You are receiving complaints from company employees regarding the pop-ads coming over the user system when connected to the network. The possible type of attack is
    A. a virus
    B. malware
    C. adware
    D. a worm

17._____

18. As a help desk operator, the employees of the organization contact you for any kind of unusual system response. On inspection, you were not able to inspect the critical elements of the virus. The reason could be that they hide themselves in some sort of protective code. The possibility could be that the virus acts as the trap and the core code is placed in some other areas of the program. What is this type of virus?
    A. Phage
    B. Companion
    C. Armored
    D. Polymorphic

18._____

19. While going through the database audit files, you come to know that some unidentified queries have been fired in order to retrieve unauthorized information. Your system is at risk for database
    A. exploitation
    B. hijacking
    C. hacking
    D. malfunctioning

19._____

20. You are performing the regular system and network scanning for the organization's workstations. While scanning, you find out that for some of the programs there exists another program having a different extension and hides in a temp directory. This associated program is executed at the time the permissible program is executed. What type of virus is it?
    A. Phage
    B. Companion
    C. Armored
    D. Polymorphic

20._____

21. A user from the organization complains about an unusual behavior of the system whenever he runs the spell checker at the time the document is opened. A macro is created whenever the user performs this action. What could be the possible type of virus attack the user is facing?
    A. Phage   B. Companion   C. Macro   D. Polymorphic

21.____

22. While going through the database inspection, you find out that there is some sort of modification not done by the authorized user. Which of the following types of virus has infected the database?
    A. Phage   B. Companion   C. Macro   D. Polymorphic

22.____

23. User A sends a message to User B. The message is 'This is my Number'. However, when User B receives the message, the text displayed was 'This is ya numba'. Which of the following types of virus has infected the communication?
    A. Phage   B. Companion   C. Macro   D. Polymorphic

23.____

24. The anti-virus installed over the system is not working appropriately. Being the help desk officer, you are receiving complaints from all the staff employees. On inspection, you find out that the anti-virus definition files are missing. Which of the following types of virus has infected the system?
    A. Phage   B. Retrovirus   C. Companion   D. Macro

24.____

25. You receive a call from an employee from your organization. He has received an e-mail which is a type of advertisement. The e-mail states to click some of the links to precede further for purchase and viewing advertisement details. Which of the following is a type of virus infection attack in this case?
    A. SPAM   B. SPIM   C. Phage   D. Trojan

25.____

KEY (CORRECT ANSWERS)

1.	C		11.	B
2.	D		12.	A
3.	D		13.	B
4.	C		14.	D
5.	C		15.	A
6.	D		16.	B
7.	A		17.	C
8.	C		18.	C
9.	D		19.	A
10.	C		20.	B

21.	C
22.	A
23.	D
24.	B
25.	A

TEST 4

Each question or incomplete statement is followed by several suggested answers or completions. Select the one that BEST answers the question or completes the statement. *PRINT THE LETTER OF THE CORRECT ANSWER IN THE SPACE AT THE RIGHT.*

1. The file virus tends to attach via the _____ file.
   A. object   B. executable   C. document   D. source

   1._____

2. Which one of the following is NOT defined as an attack, but a mechanism to check for the vulnerabilities to attacks?
   A. DoS   B. Phishing
   C. Spamming   D. Port scanning

   2._____

3. The BEST definition of the trap door is:
   A. A security hole created while programming the system
   B. An anti-virus
   C. A security hole inside the network
   D. A worm

   3._____

4. Authorization tends to deal with
   A. RSA
   B. privilege and rights
   C. three-way handshake for network communication
   D. RADIUS

   4._____

5. Which of the following makes the user to change the password after the first logon?
   A. Security policy   B. User policy
   C. System policy   D. Account administrator

   5._____

6. Which of the following is NOT a good approach when dealing with password policy?
   A. Password encryption   B. Maximum password age
   C. Change password every year   D. Delete password history

   6._____

7. Integrity breach is defined as unauthorized
   A. data destruction   B. resource utilization
   C. data reading   D. data modification

   7._____

8. Confidentiality breach is defined as unauthorized
   A. data destruction   B. resource utilization
   C. data reading   D. data modification

   8._____

9. Theft of service is defined as unauthorized
   A. data destruction   B. resource utilization
   C. data reading   D. data modification

   9._____

10. Availability breach is defined as unauthorized
    A. data destruction
    B. resource utilization
    C. data reading
    D. data modification

10._____

11. A definition of the Trojan horse is:
    A. Used for data encryption
    B. Steals for useful information
    C. It's a type of worm
    D. A rogue program that tricks user

11._____

12. A definition of a trap door is:
    A. It traps the user identification details
    B. It is a hole in software created by the designer
    C. It is a type of a virus
    D. It is a type of a worm

12._____

13. A type of method used by the worm process is _____ process.
    A. trap   B. trick   C. spawn   D. fraud

13._____

14. Which of the following is NOT defined as the virus characteristic?
    A. They destruct and alter user data
    B. Stand-alone process
    C. Code inside legitimate code
    D. It cannot be detected

14._____

15. Masquerading is defined as the process in which
    A. one party in the communication acts to be someone else
    B. both parties are legitimate
    C. attacker gains access of remote connection
    D. attacker takes over the communication between two parties

15._____

16. Which is the process of establishing boundaries for information sharing?
    A. Disassociation
    B. Compartmentalization
    C. Isolation
    D. Segregation

16._____

17. You are working as a network administrator in an organization. Your boss asks you to configure the router with a distance-vector protocol to enable classless routing. Which of the following BEST satisfies the requirement?
    A. SSH   B. OSPF   C. RADIUS   D. EIGRP

17._____

18. A call is received from the network administrator explaining that he has typed the below information into the router:
    Router(config)#router ospf 1
    Router(config-router)#network 10.0.0.0 255.0.0.0 area 0
Even after execution of the above statement, he is not able to view any routes. The mistake made by him is incorrect
    A. Wildcard mask
    B. OSPF
    C. OSPF ID
    D. AS configuration

18._____

19. You receive a call from a mobile user stating that his laptop is working
    unusually. He explains the problem by stating that it occurred when he
    downloaded a tic-tac-toe program from an untrusted website. Which of the
    following defines a program that associates with another program?
    A. Trojan horse virus   B. Polymorphic virus
    C. Worm   D. Armored virus

19.____

20. Your supervisor orders you to implement MAC filtering over the network.
    However, you do not know the MAC address of Linus based workstation. The
    type of command line tool to know the MAC address is
    A. ifconfig   B. ifconfig/show
    C. ipconfig   D. ipconfig/all

20.____

21. Two users, A and B, are communicating over the network by sharing
    legitimate authorization information. However, after some time when User B
    logs off, User A seems to still have communication with User B. What possible
    type of attack is it where the user has captured information passed between
    client server and reusing it?
    A. DoS   B. DDoS   C. Replay   D. Vishing

21.____

22. An employee from your company explains his experience with you. He wants
    to login in the HR system of the organization. When he typed in the site
    address, he was navigated to the login page. Once he entered the login info,
    the page said that invalid login info has been entered and redirects him to the
    real website page. He is worried that his credentials are stolen. What kind of
    possible attack is it?
    A. SPAM   B. Spoofing   C. Replay   D. Vishing

22.____

23. Being a network administrator, when scanning the host, you find out that in
    some cases, the user is redirected from one host to another. What is this
    specific type of situation known as?
    A. Vishing   B. Spoofing   C. Pharming   D. Replay

23.____

24. You receive a call from an employee of your company. He explains a
    situation in which a newly hired individual seems to be sneaking over his
    computer every time he enters his login information. What type of possible
    situation is the caller talking about?
    A. Tailgating   B. Shoulder surfing
    C. Vishing   D. Pharming

24.____

25. You receive a call from your supervisor to share your login details with you
    so that he can login with our credentials to perform a specific task. You avoid
    giving the details over the phone and ask to call him back. When you call back
    and ask the supervisor, he says he has not made any such call for the login
    credentials. What type of possible situation is this?
    A. Tailgating   B. Shoulder surfing
    C. Impersonation   D. Vishing

25.____

KEY (CORRECT ANSWERS)

1.	B		11.	D
2.	D		12.	B
3.	A		13.	C
4.	B		14.	D
5.	D		15.	A
6.	C		16.	B
7.	D		17.	D
8.	C		18.	A
9.	B		19.	A
10.	A		20.	A

21.	C
22.	B
23.	C
24.	B
25.	C

EXAMINATION SECTION

TEST 1

DIRECTIONS: Each question or incomplete statement is followed by several suggested answers or completions. Select the one that BEST answers the question or completes the statement. *PRINT THE LETTER OF THE CORRECT ANSWER IN THE SPACE AT THE RIGHT.*

1. Which of the following protocols tends to be unsuitable for WAN VPN connections?
   A. PPP   B. PPTP   C. L2TP   D. IPSec

   1._____

2. To cope with the possibility of recovering sensitive data from computers which are donated or thrown away by companies, which of the following security policies is adopted by the companies?
   A. Acceptable use   B. Disposal/destruction
   C. SLA   D. Privacy

   2._____

3. _____ tends to be defined as the combination of SSL and HTTP.
   A. TLS   B. DES   C. HTTPS   D. PDQ

   3._____

4. RAID _____ makes use of disk striping while using parity.
   A. 0   B. 1   C. 3   D. 5

   4._____

5. While viewing activity logs, you suspect that an attack is underway. It appears as if TCP acknowledgements are being intercepted by a hacker causing the packets to be resent and subsequently intercepted by the hacker without the receiving computer's knowledge. What type of attack is this?
   A. Back door   B. Rootkit
   C. Trojan horse   D. Replay

   5._____

6. Creating a policy which deals with how company information would be distributed and spreading the awareness among employees about the authorized personnel to deal with system and data information is effective for which type of attack?
   A. Mathematical   B. DDoS
   C. Worm   D. Social engineering

   6._____

7. Which of the following tends to be a high-availability mechanism?
   A. RAID   B. Switched networks
   C. Multiple CPU's   D. Routing tables

   7._____

8. Creating and implementing a disaster recovery plan (DRP) is mostly related to
   A. insurance coverage   B. risk assessment
   C. media spin management   D. ethical hacking

   8._____

9. Which of the following does NOT fall under physical security control?
   A. Door locks
   B. Motion detectors
   C. Bulwark
   D. Strong passwords
   9.____

10. Which of the following encryption processes makes use of one message to hide another?
    A. Steganography
    B. Hashing
    C. MDA
    D. Crypto-intelligence
    10.____

11. Which of the following is NOT a viable security option for a user currently working on a confidential document who has been informed he must attend a meeting starting in two minutes?
    A. Log off
    B. Initiate the password-protected screen saver
    C. Immediately go to the meeting
    D. Shut down the system
    11.____

12. Which type of attack uses a number of compromised hosts to focus on a single target?
    A. Hot site
    B. Phishing
    C. DDoS
    D. Targeted site
    12.____

13. What technique or method can be employed by hackers and researchers to discover unknown flaws or errors in software?
    A. Dictionary attacks
    B. Fuzzing
    C. War dialing
    D. Cross-site request forgery
    13.____

14. Which of the following is NOT a way to prevent or protect against XSS?
    A. Input validation
    B. Defensive coding
    C. Allowing script input
    D. Escaping meta-characters
    14.____

15. Which of the following is another name for social engineering?
    A. Social disguise
    B. Social hacking
    C. Wetware
    D. Wetfire
    15.____

16. The TCP/IP suite is broken into four architectural layers: Application layer, Internet layer, Network Access layer, and _____ layer.
    A. Host-to-Host or Transport
    B. Presentation
    C. Data
    D. OSI
    16.____

17. _____ is used for Web Pages and World Wide.
    A. SMTP   B. TCP   C. HTTP   S. SSL
    17.____

18. The default port for HTTPS is
    A. 443   B. 441   C. 442   D. 321
    18.____

19. _____ is defined as the software or hardware tool used in order to determine, as well as block, unwanted interactions.
    A. Firewall
    B. URL filter
    C. Spam filter
    D. Protocol analyzer

19.____

20. The Spanning Tree Protocol (STP) operates at the _____ layer and makes sure there is only one active path between two stations.
    A. Application
    B. Presentation
    C. Network
    D. Data Link

20.____

21. Pretty Good Privacy is implemented for
    A. encryption
    B. e-mail security
    C. port security
    D. authorization

21.____

22. A firewall is used to apply protection against
    A. a virus
    B. a worm
    C. malware
    D. unauthenticated logins

22.____

23. When dealing with the tunnel mode using IPSec, it is used to protect the
    A. IP header only
    B. complete message
    C. complete IP packet
    D. IP protocol

23.____

24. A _____ cloud is a mixture of private and public cloud components.
    A. private
    B. public
    C. hybrid
    D. community

24.____

25. A _____ cloud is for internal use only.
    A. hybrid
    B. public
    C. secret
    D. private

25.____

KEY (CORRECT ANSWERS)

1.	A		11.	C
2.	B		12.	C
3.	C		13.	B
4.	D		14.	C
5.	D		15.	C
6.	D		16.	A
7.	A		17.	C
8.	B		18.	A
9.	D		19.	C
10.	A		20.	D

21.	B
22.	D
23.	C
24.	C
25.	D

TEST 2

DIRECTIONS: Each question or incomplete statement is followed by several suggested answers or completions. Select the one that BEST answers the question or completes the statement. *PRINT THE LETTER OF THE CORRECT ANSWER IN THE SPACE AT THE RIGHT.*

1. _____ is the basic element utilized to establish connectivity between the two nodes.
   A. Firewall
   B. Router
   C. Switch
   D. Protocol analyzer

   1.____

2. _____ enables the groups of routers to share the routing information.
   A. Border Gateway Protocol (BGP)
   B. Routing Information Protocol (RIP)
   C. Open Shortest Path First (OSPF)
   D. Switch

   2.____

3. Two types of routes are
   A. positive and negative
   B. 0 and 1
   C. static and dynamic
   D. configured and not configured

   3.____

4. In Cisco, two main protocols are used, one being Gateway Routing Protocol (IGRP) and the other is
   A. TCP/IP
   B. SMTP
   C. UDP
   D. EIGRP

   4.____

5. Which of the following is NOT an objective of a load balancer?
   A. Minimize cost
   B. Maximize throughput
   C. Reduce overloading
   D. Eliminate bottlenecks

   5.____

6. Adware is the subset of
   A. malware
   B. spyware
   C. virus
   D. worms

   6.____

7. _____ are able to launch many DoS as well as DDoS attacks which could be in any form like adware, spyware, and spam.
   A. Botnets
   B. Worms
   C. Viruses
   D. Trojans

   7.____

8. _____ is defined as the type of malware which is intended to take control of a system to stop its usage and demanding payment for that.
   A. Malware
   B. Adware
   C. Ransomware
   D. Spyware

   8.____

9. _____ is a type of malware which hides its identification and hence makes its elimination challenging.
   A. Armored virus
   B. Polymorphic malware
   C. Adware
   D. Trojans

   9.____

10. _____ are defined as the kind of harmful code that intends to hid the recognition by means of signature.
    A. Polymorphic malware
    B. Armored virus
    C. Spyware
    D. Adware

    10.____'

11. The MOST vulnerable element when dealing with system security is   11.____
    A. information   B. people   C. software   D. hardware

12. The MOST crucial kind of loss that can be faced by an organization is of   12.____
    A. employee   B. data   C. software   D. hardware

13. _____ is defined as the recorded actions as performed by user over the   13.____
    internet.
    A. Virus   B. Worm   C. Cookie   D. Proxy

14. Antivirus is also called   14.____
    A. retrovirus   B. armored virus
    C. macro virus   D. vaccine

15. The secret keyword used to gain system access is known as   15.____
    A. IPSec   B. password
    C. private key   D. public key

16. Authentication is defined as   16.____
    A. verifying data integrity   B. verifying user identity
    C. user authorization   D. password protection

17. In cryptography, the output text is known as   17.___
    A. plain text   B. block cipher
    C. cipher text   D. encrypted text

18. Which of the following is NOT used for symmetric encryption?   18.____
    A. DES   B. SHA1   C. RC4   D. RSA

19. Protocol is defined as the   19.____
    A. rules and methods   B. rules
    C. principles   D. methods

20. The term cryptography is used to serve the purpose of   20.____
    A. testing   B. development
    C. security   D. analysis

21. The Media Access layer falls under the sub-layer of   21.____
    A. ANSI   B. ASCII
    C. IEEE   D. Data Link layer

22. SHF means   22.____
    A. Symmetric Hash Function   B. Security Hashing Field
    C. System Hashing Function   D. Symmetric Hashing Formation

23. Any loops which are created by flooding tends to be eliminated using   23.____
    A. RPF   B. SMTP   C. UDP   D. TCP

24. The routing table, which tends to be dynamic in nature, is updated
    A. instantly   B. manually   C. periodically   D. randomly

24.____

25. When dealing with IPV4, the packets which are transferred are known as
    A. spoofing   B. datagram
    C. data packets   D. data segments

25.____

————

KEY (CORRECT ANSWERS)

1.	B		11.	B
2.	A		12.	B
3.	C		13.	C
4.	D		14.	D
5.	A		15.	B
6.	B		16.	B
7.	A		17.	C
8.	C		18.	D
9.	A		19.	A
10.	A		20.	C

21.	C
22.	B
23.	A
24.	C
25.	B

————

TEST 3

DIRECTIONS: Each question or incomplete statement is followed by several suggested answers or completions. Select the one that BEST answers the question or completes the statement. *PRINT THE LETTER OF THE CORRECT ANSWER IN THE SPACE AT THE RIGHT.*

1. Round Robin is one of the techniques of
   A. Routing
   B. Load Balancing
   C. Encryption
   D. Network Security

   1.____

2. *Destination to every packet is assigned randomly.* This definition refers to which of the following techniques?
   A. Round Robin
   B. Random Choice
   C. Preferences
   D. Load Monitoring

   2.____

3. Which of the following is NOT an additional function performed by Load Balancing?
   A. Caching
   B. Secure Sockets Layer (SSL) offloading
   C. Data encapsulation
   D. Buffering

   3.____

4. NAT is defined as
   A. Network Address Translation
   B. Network Access Translation
   C. Network Access Transference
   D. Non Accessible Translation

   4.____

5. A _____ is defined as the interaction tunnel between two nodes while using an intermediate network.
   A. switch
   B. router
   C. firewall
   D. Virtual Private Network (VPN)

   5.____

6. _____ is the type of virus which transforms and changes other programs as well as databases.
   A. Stealth
   B. Phage
   C. Companion
   D. Retrovirus

   6.____

7. Those viruses which prevent their identification by masking themselves from applications are known as
   A. stealth
   B. phage
   C. companion
   D. retrovirus

   7.____

8. Which of the following are able to side step the antivirus software?
   A. Stealth
   B. Phage
   C. Companion
   D. Retrovirus

   8.____

9. The viruses which use update/software patches intended to upgrade software programs are known as
   A. macro viruses
   B. stealth
   C. phage
   D. companion

   9.____

10. _____ spoofing is NOT a type of spoofing attack.
    A. IP   B. TCP   C. ARP   D. DNS

                                                                             10.____

11. When dealing with asymmetric key cryptography, _____ keeps the private key.   11.____
    A. sender   B. both sender and receiver
    C. receiver   D. all connected to the internet

12. DES is known as Data   12.____
    A. Encryption Software   B. Encryption Solution
    C. Encapsulation Standard   D. Encryption Standard

13. DES deals with _____ cipher.   13.____
    A. block   B. brick   C. bit   D. packet

14. Cryptanalysis is defined as the process of   14.____
    A. data encryption
    B. data encapsulation
    C. data migration
    D. diagnosing insecurity within the cryptographic process

15. In order to interact with the SSH server, which of the following TCP ports is used?   15.____
    A. 21   B. 32   C. 22   D. 41

16. Decryption of the encrypted message takes place at the   16.____
    A. sender   B. receiver
    C. sender and receiver   D. intruder

17. The term DSS means Digital   17.____
    A. Standard for Security   B. System of Standards
    C. Signature System   D. Signature Standard

18. The term *One Way Authentication* is referred to as   18.____
    A. no transfer   B. double transfer
    C. half duplex transfer   D. single transfer of information

19. The term *Two Way Authentication* is referred to as   19.____
    A. no transfer   B. double transfer
    C. half duplex transfer   D. single transfer of information

20. DHCP tends to be used in order to provide _____ to the Host.   20.____
    A. URL   B. HTTP   C. IP   D. Proxy

21. IP was initially proposed to sever the purpose of   21.____
    A. tunneling   B. scheduling
    C. unicast delivery   D. multicast delivery

22. Tunneling is defined as the process used on the two systems that are operating   22.____
    A. IPV6   B. IPV2   C. IPV4   D. IPSec

23. Substitution Cipher replaces one symbol with   23.____
    A. other   B. two symbols
    C. three symbols   D. keys

24. The proxy firewall performs its actions at the _____ layer.   24.____
    A. Application   B. Datalink   C. Support   D. Presentation

25. The division of data into block as done by SSL is   25.____
    A. $2*3$ B. $2*10$ C. $2*14$ D. $2*20$

KEY (CORRECT ANSWERS)

1.	B		11.	C
2.	C		12.	D
3.	C		13.	A
4.	A		14.	D
5.	D		15.	C
6.	B		16.	B
7.	A		17.	D
8.	D		18.	D
9.	A		19.	C
10.	B		20.	C

21.	C
22.	A
23.	A
24.	A
25.	C

TEST 4

DIRECTIONS: Each question or incomplete statement is followed by several suggested answers or completions. Select the one that BEST answers the question or completes the statement. *PRINT THE LETTER OF THE CORRECT ANSWER IN THE SPACE AT THE RIGHT.*

1.   Which of the following is NOT the name of VPN Concentrator?   1.____
    A. VPN Server   B. VPN Provider
    C. VPN Gateway   D. VPN Firewall

2.   Which of the following is NOT an example of Rule Based Management Tool?   2.____
    A. Firewalls   B. Proxies   C. Routers   D. Switch

3.   _____ tends to reduce the probability of DoS attacks.   3.____
    A. Data Encapsulation   B. Encryption
    C. Flood Guard   D. Load Balancing

4.   _____ tends to act as a proxy among the local area network and the internet.   4.____
    A. NAT   B. VPN   C. IPSec   D. Router

5.   Which of the following is NOT the area in which virtualization can be   5.____
implemented?
    A. Server   B. Application
    C. Presentation   D. Network

6.   _____ deals with the actual danger under consideration.   6.____
    A. Risk   B. Threat   C. Vulnerability   D. Virus

7.   _____ deals with likely causes associated with the risk.   7.____
    A. Risk   B. Threat   C. Vulnerability   D. Virus

8.   _____ deals with where the system is weak.   8.____
    A. Risk   B. Threat   C. Vulnerability   D. Virus

9.   Which of the following is an attack in which a hacker configures his or her   9.____
system as a twin of the legitimate wireless access point?
    A. Evil Twin   B. War Diving
    C. Bluejacking   D. Packet Sniffing

10. Which of the following is regarded as spam over IM?   10.____
    A. IP spoofing   B. DNS spoofing
    C. Spim   D. Phishing

11. SSH-2 lacks which of the following layers?   11.____
    A. Transport   B. Physical
    C. Connection   D. User Authentication

12. SCP is the protocol which is based on which of the following over SSH?   12.____
    A. SMTP   B. TCP   C. RCP   D. DHCP

13. Which of the following TCP ports is used by SMTP?   13.____
    A. 25   B. 35   C. 45   D. 55

14. SMTP is used for message   14.____
    A. transport   B. encryption   C. content   D. delivery

15. FTP makes use of how many TCP connections that are running in parallel for file transfer?   15.____
    A. 2   B. 4   C. 6   D. 8

16. DHCP tends to make use of port _____ for sending information.   16.____
    A. 62   B. 63   C. 65   D. 67

17. While communicating on the same subnet, DHCP client and server use   17.____
    A. UDP Broadcast   B. TCP Broadcast
    C. SMTP   D. FTP

18. When the IP address is achieved, which of the following is used in order to be able to avoid IP conflict?   18.____
    A. Address resolution protocol   B. IP conflict resolution
    C. Changing the IP address   D. Gateway protocol

19. The protocol ICMP tends to be utilized for   19.____
    A. Ifconfig   B. Traceroute
    C. Ping   D. Ping and Traceroute

20. The process of signing the message while sending is known as   20.____
    A. Digital System   B. Digital Signature
    C. Digital Text   D. Encryption

21. When working with an asymmetric key, _____ key is used.   21.____
    A. 2   B. 3   C. 4   D. 5

22. SNMP exists in _____ versions.   22.____
    A. 3   B. 4   C. 5   D. 2

23. SNMPv3 has improved _____ compared to SNMPv2.   23.____
    A. speed   B. precision   C. security   D. accuracy

24. The SHA-1 consists of a message comprising _____ bits.   24.____
    A. 1000   B. 512   C. 820   D. 160

25. _____ Cipher is referred to as the Transposition Cipher.   25.____
    A. Block   b. Playfair   C. Caesar   D. Multi

KEY (CORRECT ANSWERS)

1.	B		11.	B
2.	D		12.	C
3.	C		13.	A
4.	A		14.	A
5.	D		15.	A
6.	A		16.	D
7.	B		17.	A
8.	C		18.	A
9.	A		19.	D
10.	C		20.	B

21.	A
22.	D
23.	C
24.	D
25.	B

Made in the USA
Coppell, TX
07 June 2021